"This powerful and transformative guide is a must-read for those seeking to thri
offering a road map to dismantle barriers and respond effectively to anti-Black ra
sparks introspection, and unveils practical strategies for resilience by offering ke
advice through the application of the SNAPS (Strategically Navigating Anti-Black Racism in Professional
Spaces) decision making model to help uplift Black professionals to assert their presence in professional
spaces."

> —**Terrill O. Taylor, PhD**, assistant professor of psychology at the University of Maryland,
> College Park

"Rooted in the science of Black psychology, Pearis L. Jean's groundbreaking SNAPS decision making
model empowers us with the self-knowledge, confidence, and tools to respond to workplace anti-Black
racism in ways that honor our personal and professional values. Racial trauma's impact on our energy,
functioning, and well-being often goes unnoticed. This exceptional resource provides powerful exercises,
relatable stories, and targeted activities to help readers develop crucial skills in addressing the effects of
racial trauma."

> —**Robyn L. Gobin, PhD**, licensed psychologist, associate professor at the University of Illinois
> at Urbana–Champaign, and author of *The Self-Care Prescription* and *The Black Woman's
> Guide to Overcoming Domestic Violence*

"*Strategically Navigating Anti-Black Racism in Professional Spaces* is brilliantly composed and effortlessly
accessible to its audience. This workbook skillfully leads readers through the tapestry of historical context,
intricate concepts, and engaging activities—presenting concrete solutions for tackling anti-Black racism
in professional spheres and broader society. It's an essential resource for Black folx and those dedicated
to their liberation and well-being, marking it as an unequivocal imperative for anyone poised to ignite
transformative change."

> —**Maryam Jernigan-Noesi, PhD**, licensed psychologist, educator, and consultant with expertise
> in racial stress and trauma across the lifespan and racial justice

"Pearis L. Jean's book is a practical and thoughtful manual for what to do when encountering anti-Black racism at work, urging readers to interrogate their own values and goals at the onset. This guidebook should be required reading for early-career Black professionals, and offers more tenured professionals a therapeutic outlet to process their own workplace trauma, as well as develop better strategies for handling anti-Black racism in the future."

—**Joi Louviere**, creator and host of the *Werk Stories* podcast, a show that explores the workplace experiences of women of color through intimate one-on-one interviews

"Pearis Jean has done the remarkable work of producing a balm in the face of anti-Black racism rooted in the revolutionary, loving, and intimate traditions of Black peoples. This book has the potential to not only advance the survival of Black people, but also offer practical tools for immediate safety as well as for creative resistance. The SNAPS model lights a path to our own collective exultation."

—**Evan Auguste, PhD**, assistant professor at UMass Boston

"This book is a must-read for anyone who has ever experienced racial (micro)aggression. Pearis Jean has provided tools on how to speak to them and heal from them. She explores ways to know racial identity and racial socialization better, and how to better improve our mental health."

—**Shareefah Al'Uqdah**, associate professor, and chief psychologist at Your Neighborhood Clinic

The Social Justice Handbook Series

As culture evolves, we need new tools to help us cope and interact with our social world in ways that feel authentic and empowered. That's why New Harbinger created the *Social Justice Handbook* series—a series that teaches readers how to use practical, psychology-based tools to challenge and transform dominant culture, both in their daily lives and in their communities.

Written by thought leaders in the fields of psychology, sociology, gender, and ethnic studies, the *Social Justice Handbook* series offers evidence-based strategies for coping with a broad range of social inequities that impact quality of life. As research has shown us, social oppression can lead to mental health issues such as depression, anxiety, trauma, lowered self-esteem, and self-harm. These handbooks provide accessible social analysis as well as thoughtful activities and exercises based on the latest psychological methods to help readers unlearn internalized negative messages, resist social inequities, transform their communities, and challenge dominant culture to be equitable for all.

The handbooks also serve as a hands-on resource for therapists who wish to integrate an understanding and acknowledgment of how multiple social issues impact their clients to provide relevant and supportive care.

For a complete list of books in
the *Social Justice Handbook* series,
visit newharbinger.com

Strategically Navigating Anti-Black Racism *in* Professional Spaces

A Practical Guide for Black People Responding to Racism in the Workplace

PEARIS L. JEAN, PHD

New Harbinger Publications, Inc.

Publisher's Note

NEW HARBINGER PUBLICATIONS is a registered trademark of New Harbinger Publications, Inc.

New Harbinger Publications is an employee-owned company.

Copyright © 2024 by Pearis L. Jean
New Harbinger Publications, Inc.
5720 Shattuck Avenue
Oakland, CA 94609
www.newharbinger.com

Cover design by Amy Daniel

Acquired by Jennye Garibaldi

Edited by Diedre Hammons

Library of Congress Cataloging-in-Publication Data on file

Printed in the United States of America

26   25   24

10   9   8   7   6   5   4   3   2   1   First Printing

Contents

Acknowledgments

I want to first give honor and thanks to God.

Thank you to my ancestors for having enough hope for the future to have the next generation. Thank you to my loved ones and elders turned ancestors. Although you are no longer here, your memory will always live on within me. Thank you to my husband, family (chosen and biological), friends, mentors, and loved ones.

Thank you to every Black person who I have crossed paths with whether through school, career, clinical work, research, or another domain of life.

To every Black person who has experienced anti-Black racism, it is not your fault. We should not have to deal with the racism we experience and yet we do. This book is to get us through with hope for a liberated future where there is no racism to respond to.

Foreword

Racism remains a formidable trap, one that entangles and constricts, hindering the paths of Black professionals as they navigate both external challenges and their inner worlds. Dr. Pearis L. Jean has crafted a transformative workbook, akin to a well-crafted map, serving as a guiding light for those maneuvering the tightrope between dignity and success in the spaces where they earn and learn. This book's precision in addressing the complexities of anti-Black racism within professional spheres provides a focused lens through which to navigate these fraught experiences.

For Black individuals in the United States, the term "professional" carries profound historical weight. It embodies a narrative of forced inclusion, exclusion, and the creation of our own professions, woven deeply into the fabric of our Black identity. Yet, within the confines of a culture steeped in white supremacy, pursuing our professions and "professionalism" often births toxic environments for Black individuals. The resulting stress and interpersonal challenges in our workplaces and educational spaces are burdensome. We spend significant portions of our lives in these domains and deserve to cultivate wellness there.

Dr. Jean's work emphasizes the importance of prioritizing prevention planning. By preparing us to respond proactively and advocating for the development of strategies well before encountering racism or violence, this workbook equips us to navigate these moments with presence and purpose. In the throes of anti-Blackness, when thoughts swirl and actions seem elusive, these strategies offer a lifeline, enhancing our ability to engage meaningfully in those crucial moments.

Having collaborated closely with Dr. Jean throughout her extensive three-year journey in formulating the strategically navigating anti-Black racism in professional spaces (SNAPS) model, I witnessed the birth of powerful questions: What informs the decision making processes of Black graduate students and early-career professionals in response to anti-Black racism? What are the consequences, perceived or experienced, of these responses? What strategies do these individuals consider most effective? Through meticulous interviews with Black professionals at various career stages, Dr. Jean and her team crafted, refined, and honed this decision making model to its current form—a text that empowers individuals with critical and deliberate strategies to persevere following racist encounters.

Many of us yearn to be prepared for the battles we know are all too likely. Yet, who offers guidance for these fights? SNAPS is a strategy tailored by a young Black professional for young Black professionals, rooted not just in a shared experience of racial trauma but in the depths of psychology research on racial trauma and Black wellness. Beyond shared identity and research skillfulness, Dr. Jean is a principled leader and healer, accountable to her communities, which imbues this offering with authenticity and depth.

Furthermore, as a public educator and university professor, her teaching methodology transforms this workbook into a journey of healing and learning, empowering readers to emerge more grounded, equipped, and ready to face internal and interpersonal battles.

Rest assured, Dr. Jean's thoroughness, guided by a Black feminist love ethic, permeates this workbook. Beyond providing a blueprint for navigating racism, it offers scripts for responding to racism, her own personal narratives, prolific case studies, cutting-edge psychoeducation, an integration of African and Black American history, and heartfelt encouragement. The process itself also mirrors this thoroughness, gently yet critically guiding readers on a journey towards tightened strategies and expanded pathways to confront racism and heal racial trauma.

For the intellectuals, the creatives, those simply trying to do their jobs, and all the contemplative souls wrestling with racism or anxiety born from resistance, the SNAPS workbook is a sanctuary—a place for respite, release, and perhaps even joy. It invites readers to delve into their inner landscapes while connecting with the external reality of racism, all through a lens focused on healing and trauma-informed care. Engaging with these pages is an intimate and brave act, a necessary spiritual endeavor that nurtures self-discovery and safeguards the heart and body, promoting wellness in professional and educational spaces.

This book is offered as a preventive tool against the realities of racial trauma and its associated psychosocial and physiological consequences. As we break the curses of generational trauma, may our ancestors find peace, and may the truths encapsulated within these pages serve as a healing balm for all who engage with them.

—Della V. Mosely, PhD
   President of the WELLS Healing Center

Introduction

Have you ever been in a situation where a colleague says something racist to you in a professional setting? Maybe your colleague confused you for another Black person at your job, mispronounced your name, touched your hair, or made a derogatory comment about Black people during a meeting. *How did you feel in that situation? What thoughts went through your mind?*

You may have had a rush of different thoughts ranging from "I am not about to let this person play me like this" to "Oh, yeah, I am at work and need to calm down." Physically, you may notice that your shoulders tense up and your jaw clenches. You may notice that your mind is racing, or your mind goes blank. You may feel like the room is getting hotter and start to sweat or you may notice your head or stomach starts to hurt. You may experience other thoughts, emotions, and physical reactions that differ from what I described.

Researchers have found that Black people often feel "frozen" during situations of anti-Black racism in the workplace (Dickens and Chavez 2018). During those moments, you may wonder what you should do and find yourself considering all sorts of options. These situations are often dysregulating and can ruin an otherwise great day. This book is intended to allow you to think through your decision making when (a) responding to racism in a professional space before anything even happens, (b) responding when something has happened, and (c) planning your next steps after something has happened.

If you have ever experienced racism in your workplace, academic setting, networking event, or other professional setting, then this book is for you. If you have wondered how to respond when someone says or does something anti-Black, then this book is for you. If you want to respond to anti-Black racism in ways that align with your wellness and values, then this book is for you. The focus of this book is on the interpersonal level of racism and specifically the decision making process that Black professionals face when responding to interpersonal racist incidents. We should not have to deal with the racism we experience in our professional spaces or personal lives, but unfortunately, experiencing racism is a reality for many of us. This book is intended to aid you in *strategically navigating anti-Black racism in professional spaces* (SNAPS) in ways that align with who you are and what you hope to gain from the space.

Oftentimes, after a racist incident like a coworker touching your hair or a manager remarking that you are surprisingly articulate, we will wish we said "this" or regret that we did "that"; this book is intended to provide you with a structure and way of thinking through your responses to anti-Black racism so that no matter how the other person reacts, you can stand firm and proud in your response. So, let's talk about it: what is anti-Black racism and what impact can anti-Black racism have on our psychological well-being?

Anti-Black Racism in All Its Forms

In her book, *Unapologetic: A Black, Queer, and Feminist Mandate for Radical Movements*, Charlene Carruthers defines anti-Black racism (ABR) as, "the system of beliefs and practices that attack, erode, and limit the humanity of Black people" (Carruthers 2018, 26). ABR describes the unique racism that Black people experience and acknowledges the specificity of our experiences of oppression. Continuous exposure to ABR from a multitude of sources can lead to racial trauma for individuals. Racial trauma, also known as race-based traumatic stress, is described by researchers like Thema Bryant and Robert Carter as psychological, emotional, and physical harm that Black and other people of color (POC) experience from real or perceived racism (i.e., overt, covert, systemic racism) (Bryant-Davis and Ocampo 2005; Carter 2007).

Racial trauma is cumulative and can cause symptoms like re-experiencing trauma, avoidance, arousal, and negative mood and thoughts. For example, racial trauma may look like you no longer attending (i.e., avoidance) holiday parties hosted by your job because of repeated incidences of your colleagues singing along to certain songs that include the N-word. The harmful effects of ABR are evident throughout history, but Black people have found many ways to resist ABR and cope with racial trauma. This book is meant to be another tool that you can use to resist ABR in professional spaces.

History of Anti-Black Racism in the United States

The United States has a long history of racism including the perpetuation of a social hierarchy based on race. The theft of Indigenous lands and resources along with the enslavement of African people in the United States from 1619 to 1865 by European colonizers laid the foundation for our current racialized society. For some of you, you are the descendants of enslaved Africans in the United States and have had to navigate oppressive systems that were developed based on the disenfranchisement of your ancestors. For others, you or your family may have immigrated to the United States in recent generations and have had to adjust to the racialized nuances and dynamics of the United States. Either way, you likely have experienced ABR in your personal and professional life. In this book, we will discuss what ABR looks like on the interpersonal level and how that affects our responses to ABR in the workplace.

Despite oppressive systems and racist people, Black people have resisted ABR from the beginning of their interactions with white colonizers. For example, African cultural roles (i.e., recorder, interpreter, creator, advancer, maintainer, and memorializer) were used by enslaved Africans to make sense of the United States (Asante 2021). Enslaved Africans in the United States, Caribbean, and South America used these roles to immediately respond to their new reality of white violence and subjugation by relying on the strength of their African roots. This early form of resistance through cultural knowledge, strategy, and survival laid the groundwork for how we would continue to resist white supremacist violence in its many forms throughout history.

As a result, from the Haitian Revolution to Nat Turner's Rebellion to the Civil Rights Movement to the Black Panthers to the Movement for Black Lives, Black people throughout history have had to make crucial and often swift decisions about how to combat ABR. We can learn from them that there are a variety of ways to respond to ABR that are based on our personal experiences and values as well as our short-term and long-term goals. The Civil Rights Movement is an example of the various decisions Black people made when deciding to respond to ABR. Leaders like Dr. Martin Luther King Jr., Rosa Parks, Ella Baker, Fannie Lou Hamer, John Lewis, and others relied on strategic and peaceful methods of resistance including sit-ins, marches, and boycotts. Other leaders like Malcolm X, members of the Nation of Islam, and the Black Power Movement responded to ABR by creating their own programs to address the unmet needs of the Black community due to systemic racism. They also defended themselves against violent attacks and directly called out the harm done to Black people by white people.

History often juxtaposes leaders like Dr. Martin Luther King Jr. and Malcolm X and often uplifts one over the other. However, when I think of these leaders and ancestors, I see the different decision making processes that Black leaders of that time underwent when responding to ABR. Their responses were heavily influenced by their life experiences, values of their community, socialization, and vision for the Black community. *Black ancestors and present-day leaders did not provide one blueprint for how to respond to ABR and oppression but rather have left varied and divergent pathways for us to either follow or choose to make our own.* We stand on the shoulders of our ancestors' sacrifices. And although our challenges may be different, there are lessons that we can learn from looking to their decision making and responses to ABR.

ACTIVITY
Learning from History

Use the table below to name three Black historical figures or groups who had to make decisions about how to respond to ABR. Reflect on how their decision making style and approach may align with or not align with how you approach decision making. When thinking about historical figures, feel free to think about family members or local heroes. If you find yourself struggling to think of historical figures, check out the Further Reading and Additional Resources section in the back of this book for some inspiration.

Historical Figure or Group	Time Period and Situation of ABR	How Did They Respond?	What Did They Consider? What Can You Learn?
Dr. Martin Luther King	1950s and 1960s; Civil Rights Movement	Boycotts, protests, encouraging government officials to make policy change; reliance on teachings of Christianity	His socialization as a Christan and minister; access to government officials and how he used his privilege to advocate for change

Historical Figure or Group	Time Period and Situation of ABR	How Did They Respond?	What Did They Consider? What Can You Learn?

Types of Racism

Many people have difficulty recognizing and then responding to ABR due to the varied ways that racism can manifest. Understanding the different types of ABR can allow you to better identify ABR and think through responses that best address the ABR. Also, when we are able to name and identify the racism we are experiencing, we can feel validated.

The social psychologist James M. Jones introduced names and definitions for types of racism and other scholars have expanded on the four categories (Jones 1981). The four categories are individual or everyday racism, institutional racism, cultural racism, and environmental racism. When we can identify the types of racism that we are experiencing, we are able to think of responses on the individual, community, and societal level to combat the oppression we are experiencing. Additionally, when we can identify the type of racism we are experiencing, we will be less tempted to blame ourselves for situations and experiences that are beyond our control because we have a name for the oppression that we are experiencing.

ACTIVITY
The Different Manifestations of Racism

See the table below for definitions of each type of racism and examples. Think about which form of racism you have experienced the most and add more examples, if you can, from your own life, the lives of people around you, or from the media.

Interpersonal Racism	Institutional Racism	Cultural Racism	Environmental Racism
Personal acts done to an individual. *You may experience this type of racism during interactions with coworkers.*	Systemic racism including practices, norms, and policies that perpetuate inequity. *You may experience this type of racism in your institution and field's policies and company culture. You also may see this type of racism reflected in who is hired and in leadership at your company.*	Devaluing and "othering" cultures that differ from white culture. *You may experience this in your company's culture. Your company may only provide days off for Christian holidays.*	Environmental policies and life-threatening pollutants that are present in communities of color. *You may notice that majority Black, Indigenous, and people of color cities and towns are exposed to more pollutants and fewer resources.*
Example: Microaggressions are a type of individual racism, which includes daily racial insults. Microaggressions are often unclear and indirect and can create uncertainty among the people experiencing them about whether they are experiencing racism.	**Example:** Black people are often imprisoned and given harsher and longer sentences than white people who have committed similar crimes.	**Example:** The expectation for immigrants to the United States to speak English despite the United States not having an official language.	**Example:** The Flint water crisis (starting in 2014) where the water supply of the majority-Black town of Flint, Michigan, was contaminated, and government officials mishandled the crisis.

Interpersonal Racism	Institutional Racism	Cultural Racism	Environmental Racism

Racism manifests in a variety of ways, in addition to the types of racism listed above. Racist incidents can be intentional or unintentional, systemic or random, individual or institutional, but often lead to a similar outcome: harm to the victims of such incidents.

We can also experience perceived racism, which is a subjective experience of prejudice or discrimination. This type of racism can be so nuanced that some Black people often report feeling "crazy" trying to determine if the situation is racism and how they should respond (Gildersleeve, Croom, and Vasquez 2011). This can look like noticing that your manager only asks you to work on projects related to diversity, which you are interested in, but you have noticed that these projects do not receive the same amount of resources or support from the company. In contrast, your non-Black coworkers are given projects related to their interests and areas of expertise and are never put on the diversity-related projects. In this situation, you may feel hesitant to call this ABR because you enjoy the work you are doing with the diversity-related projects and your manager has not explicitly said that they only give these projects to Black people in the company. You may feel that something is off but may struggle to put into words what is happening or struggle to identify how you want to respond. Specifically, in workplaces, feelings of uncertainty in how to respond to racism are even more present because of the commonality and insidious nature of racism, white supremacy culture (see "Further Reading"), and politics in the workplace.

The Psychological Effects of Racism: Racial Trauma

Historically, responding to ABR has come with dire and brutalizing consequences (e.g., whippings, lynchings, separation of families, and assaults). Those consequences of responding are still present today, but more often, the consequences are more subtle and insidious. Calling out racism in your workplace can lead to social isolation from individuals with privileged identities who aim to punish marginalized individuals for challenging the workplace culture. Additionally, you may face retaliation from your superiors (i.e., advisers, supervisors, and managers). Retaliation may come in being passed over for promotions, negative evaluations, smear campaigns to others in your field, and even being removed from your position. The threats of retaliation for challenging the dominant culture can have economic, psychological, physiological, and spiritual effects on a person.

Psychologically, the impact of experiencing ABR and the subsequent retaliation from responding to perpetrators of ABR can lead to racial trauma. Racial trauma symptoms share some similarity with post-traumatic stress disorder including feelings of regret, shame, fear, embarrassment, anger, depression, anxiety, and mistrust (Bryant-Davis and Ocampo 2005; Comas-Díaz, Hall, and Neville 2019). Responding to ABR, especially on the interpersonal level, is scary, and just experiencing a racist incident can have a substantial impact on our mental health and well-being. We do not know how people will respond and we often have seen how others who push back against racism are treated. It can feel like a daunting task when we think about how to address the harm of ABR while also knowing that we live in a society that devalues and harms Black people.

I can imagine as you read through this introduction that you are wondering what you will be asked to do in this book and if this book can really help you. These are valid concerns. I wrote this book because so many of us have to navigate anti-Blackness in our workplaces and are often so isolated that we have limited resources to support us. My intention with this book is to give you the tools to respond to ABR when it shows up at work and in your life so that you can protect your mental and physical wellness. Because contrary to what society tries to tell us, we are valuable and our wellness is important.

How to Use This Book

This book will walk you through the strategically navigating anti-Black racism in professional spaces (SNAPS) decision making model. You will learn about each component of the SNAPS decision making model and through various reflection questions and activities be able to identify how the model can aid you when you are deciding how to respond to ABR in professional spaces. Feel free to write in this book (there is space), but also keep a journal nearby in case the reflection questions inspire you to write more. This book is not designed to be read in one day but is designed to be a resource that you return to at different stages of your life. Take your time, listen to your mind and body, and be open to where this journey takes you.

I also encourage you to find ways to be in community with other Black folks who may be working through the book. Come together and share your reflections and responses. We do not have to navigate ABR alone. Think of this book not only as a companion that you can look to when you are feeling isolated and confused but also use this book as an opportunity to have important conversations with those in your life that may lead to insights and revelations that you could not have imagined.

Throughout this book, short stories at the end of each chapter will be used to illustrate the SNAPS decision making model and the focus of the chapter. The stories will allow you to see how each part of the model can be used when deciding how to respond to interpersonal ABR in the workplace. Please note that these stories are merely meant to serve as examples of how the model can be used and the responses are meant to exemplify the variety of responses Black people can have to ABR. These are not stories about specific people but are composites of common experiences of Black people in professional spaces. Feel free to agree, disagree, and even rewrite the stories in ways that feel most accurate and applicable to you.

Self-Reflection Questions

Throughout each chapter, you will be asked to take some time to reflect on the contents of the chapter. In each chapter, you will find reflection questions, surveys, and activities related to the contents of the chapter. Feel free to take your time and even leave room for how your responses to each question may change over time. There are no right or wrong answers, so stay attuned to the emotions, thoughts, and reactions that come up for you as you move through this book. Also, experiences of discrimination such as ABR can significantly affect your mental health. Although this book can be a part of your mental health journey, this book is not a substitute for working with a licensed mental health professional.

Speaking of reflection questions and activities, here are some below. Think about who you are and what you want to get out of this book.

Reflection Questions

Why did you purchase this book or why do you think someone else purchased this book for you? What do you hope to gain from this book?

_____

_____

_____

_____

_____

_____

ACTIVITY

Think about your past experiences of ABR and the responses that you have had in the past. Use the graphic below to identify at least three experiences that you feel had a significant impact on you.

	Age	Experience	Setting	Type of Racism	Response	Current Impact
Experience #1						
Experience #2						
Experience #3						

If you are Black in America, it is highly unlikely that you have not experienced some form of racism throughout your life. I hate that you had to go through that. The activity above allows you to think about the anti-Black incidents that may have shaped and affected how you navigate ABR today. If no one has said this to you, let me say it: you should not have had to experience that, and it is not your fault. Thinking about those experiences probably brought up a lot of uncomfortable emotions. Feel free to take a break, do something you enjoy, get some fresh air, or take care of yourself in another way that feels good to you. When you are ready to return, we will talk about the SNAPS decision making model and how you can use it to strategically navigate ABR in the workplace.

CHAPTER 1

The SNAPS Decision Making Model

In this chapter, you can expect to:

✓ Learn about historically anti-Black stereotypes and tropes as well as explore how these stereotypes can show up in the workplace and may impact your responses to anti-Black racism

✓ Learn about the components of the SNAPS decision making model

✓ Reflect on experiences of anti-Black racism that may have influenced your decision to read this book

After graduating from a historically Black university, I did not realize how different my experiences would be while attending graduate school at a predominately white university. I felt equipped with the confidence from my undergrad experience, but I was not prepared for how difficult and out of practice I was with navigating anti-Black environments. I often found myself second-guessing my experiences and questioning if I should have responded differently or even reacted at all.

Once, a classmate of mine was invoking anti-Black stereotypes in class and using her privilege as a white woman to undermine our Black professor. I named what she was doing as anti-Black and identified specifically what was inappropriate about her statements. I was met with tears and accusations that I was "aggressive" and "mean." I noticed my non-Black peers coming to her aid while the facilitator urged me to respond "professionally" even though the white woman was crying, cursing, and continuing to be anti-Black. I left the interaction frustrated and drained as a Black woman counseling psychology student. I was confronted with being viewed as the aggressor even when I was ascribing to our asserted social justice values.

In that moment and many moments after that, I yearned for a decision making model. I wanted to have some way of assessing the situation and making a decision on how to respond that would not lead to me feeling like crap or my coworkers thinking they could just be racist whenever they wanted. I realized that it is hard to experience ABR in professional spaces and even harder to discern the most appropriate response.

One of the more dehumanizing aspects of ABR is feeling like you are stripped of your humanity. Oftentimes, when we experience ABR in professional spaces, anti-Black stereotypes are projected onto us without any regard for our individual personality traits. For me, it often has been that I'm an "angry Black woman," a "Black superwoman," a "mammy," or even at times oversexualized and considered a "Jezebel." I often felt like I had to walk a tightrope between my genuine reactions to situations of ABR and the anti-Black stereotypes that were used to negate my responses. I began to wonder: *How can I decide to respond to ABR in a way that supports my emotional and mental health while ensuring I can meet my professional goals and aspirations?*

Common Anti-Black Stereotypes

Before we can decide to respond, it's important to know and reflect on the common anti-Black stereotypes that are used to perpetuate harm toward us. These stereotypes have been used for hundreds of years to perpetuate anti-Blackness and are important to acknowledge when we think about how we respond because they often influence how non-Black people view us. Review the common anti-Black stereotype descriptions (many originated during slavery and can still be seen in media portrayals) and think of how you feel when these stereotypes are attributed to you by others (Fain 2015; Gilliam 1999; Glenn and Cunningham, 2009; Reynolds-Dobbs, Thomas, and Harrison 2008).

Stereotype	Characteristics	Reflections
Mammy	Originated from slavery to show that Black people were content with slavery Often described as dark-skinned and overweight Motherly Loyal Self-sacrificing Nurturing Not viewed as a sexual being	

Stereotype	Characteristics	Reflections
Jezebel	Originated in slavery to rationalize the rape of Black women who were enslaved Often attributed to fair-skinned/ biracial women Seductive Temptress Manipulative Hypersexual	
Sapphire	Loud Talkative Dramatic Bossy Complainer Sassy	
Crazy Black "B"	Emotionally volatile Overly aggressive and argumentative Untrustworthy Sometimes depicted as unprofessional and lazy Difficulty keeping relationships Will do anything to achieve success	

Stereotype	Characteristics	Reflections
Superwoman	Highly educated Middle class Can handle large amounts of distasteful work Does not have the same fears, insecurities, and weaknesses as other women	
The Welfare Queen	Originated during campaign speeches by former president Ronald Reagan Lazy Poor Takes advantage of government programs Unwed Possibly abusive or neglectful to her children Reinforces false stereotype held by white people that Black people are the majority of welfare recipients.	
Magical Negro	Helpful character in movies and shows Can be any gender Helps the white protagonists with wisdom or spirituality Gives the white protagonist some "soul" Can appear as a spirit or an angel Uses their powers to help the white protagonist, but not themselves	

Stereotype	Characteristics	Reflections
Uncle Tom	Originated from Harriet Beecher Stowe's 1852 book, *Uncle Tom's Cabin* Kind and benevolent Submissive and obedient Desires white approval	
Mandingo (the Black Buck)	Originated during slavery Young and muscular Limited intellect and able to be controlled Viewed as a breeder for slave masters Post-slavery: Black men were portrayed and viewed as animalistic and brutish Stereotype used to validate lynchings of Black men because of fear that they would harm white women Present day: Can be seen in white and non-Black women's fetishization of Black men, especially athletes and other celebrities	
Sambo	Originated from the 1898 children's book *The Story of Little Black Sambo* by Helen Bannerman Extremely happy Carefree Lazy Irresponsible Comedic relief Sidekick	

Reflection Questions

1. Which of these characteristics or stereotypes have been attributed to you?

    _____

    _____

    _____

2. How have you seen these stereotypes show up in the workplace?

    _____

    _____

    _____

3. How did those situations make you feel?

    _____

    _____

    _____

The SNAPS Decision Making Model

Unfortunately, ABR happens—and it happens to many of us. And when it happens, it hurts us. ABR hurts our mental health. ABR hurts our dreams. The SNAPS decision making model allows us to feel prepared for these experiences and aware of how ABR can affect our wellness.

So, let's break down the SNAPS decision making model. The model can be described as "playing chess, not checkers." Chess requires forethought and strategy, each piece having a unique role and skill set. In contrast, checkers relies less on advanced strategy; each piece has the same role and skill set.

Historically, those in power have used strategy to oppress Black people and try to minimize our gains. Therefore, institutions such as companies and schools were built around the exclusion and disdain for Black people and continue to operate within their anti-Black roots. That means we must use strategy to protect our wellness and goals. Like chess, we have to find key players that we can use to our advantage (i.e., allies, accomplices, and advocates) and identify adversaries/opponents (i.e., anti-Black subordinates, coworkers, and managers). Competitive chess players practice to hone their craft and anticipate and prepare for complex situations. For us, strategically navigating ABR is more than a "craft" but a way of protecting ourselves from the frozen feeling and racial trauma that ensues during and after an experience of ABR.

I've developed a framework to support you when you're experiencing racism in the workplace, at school, or in other professional settings. This will help you make informed decisions about how to respond to ABR in ways that align with your personal and professional values and goals. The SNAPS (strategically navigating anti-Black racism in professional spaces) decision making model applies to three domains or stages of decision making (i.e., pre-incident, incident, and post-incident decisions).

Table 1A

	Situation	Decisions to Be Made	Questions to Address
Pre-Incident	You are new to your job, getting acquainted with your coworkers and managers.	How to prepare and anticipate racial trauma and, ideally, mitigate its impact on your personal and professional wellness.	How can you emotionally, mentally, and physically prepare yourself for experiences of ABR in your workplace?
Incident	ABR occurs. A subordinate, coworker, or manager makes an anti-Black comment or behaves in a way that makes you uncomfortable.	An in-the-moment decision about how to respond or not respond.	How do you decide how to respond in the moment after an instance of interpersonal ABR?
Post-Incident	Workplace racism continues. You notice yourself feeling anxious when you have to interact with people. You struggle to cope with the culminating effects of the interpersonal ABR that you experience.	How to process, strategize, and respond in the long-term after the anti-Black incident.	How do you respond and take care of yourself after an instance of interpersonal ABR?

ACTIVITY
Reflecting on Experiences of ABR

Think about a time that you experienced ABR. What was going on in your life pre-incident? What happened during the incident? What happened after the incident of ABR? Were there decisions that you made pre-incident, during the incident, and post-incident that influenced how you responded? Use the chart below to think of your own experiences and the decisions that you may need to make in each situation. Reflect on the experiences of others as well.

	Pre-Incident	Incident	Post-Incident
Personal Example Situation			
Decisions to Be Made in Each Situation			

Reflection Questions

1. When you have experienced ABR in a professional setting, were there any indications that something like that would happen?

   _____

   _____

   _____

2. What are some things that you can do before you even experience ABR in the workplace that may prepare you to make decisions that are best for you?

   _____

   _____

   _____

3. What might be the benefits of having a plan for navigating ABR in your workplace even before you experience ABR?

   _____

   _____

   _____

Strategically Navigating ABR

Strategically navigating ABR refers to the ability to observe, collect, and analyze personal and situational data about your workplace environment. This process involves being aware of your social identities and emotional and mental capacity (i.e., past experiences of racial trauma and/or any pre-existing mental health conditions) as well as being aware of those around you and the dynamics of your workplace. Essentially, this approach encourages you to develop a curiosity for yourself and about those around you so that you can make informed decisions as you navigate your workplace. In this book, we will progress through a framework of strategically navigating ABR, chapter by chapter. Each chapter will cover these strategies in depth.

Further, it is important to be *mindful of your long-term goals and intentions* in your workplace environment as well as your *level of connectedness and responsibility to the Black community and broader POC community*. You then use this information to define and *assess your survival and safety* as you navigate your workplace. In addition to your personal information, this model involves incorporating information from various situations in your workplace. This includes *assessing the likelihood of change* based on your response to ABR, data from other Black people or marginalized individuals who have spoken up in the past, your past experiences, identifying who can be trusted, and determining the best way to convey your response with an awareness of anti-Black tropes and stereotypes that may be projected onto you when you respond.

Strategically navigating ABR incorporates the conscious and unconscious ways that Black people obtain, analyze, and act on information about themselves and the settings that they occupy to minimize harm (e.g., retaliation, financial and career impacts) and maximize benefits for our personally defined values and goals. Strategically navigating ABR is not only focused on your immediate reaction in the moment but also requires preparation and forethought pre-incident, during the incident, and post-incident. This approach to responding to ABR is not stepwise but requires mindfulness of self, others, and environment to respond in a way that most aligns with your values, goals, and wellness. The core of this strategy is *knowledge of self*, which is how who we are influences how we approach the other components of the model and make decisions. Additionally, knowledge of self is a vital part of Black psychology.

The model and description of the components of the model are below:

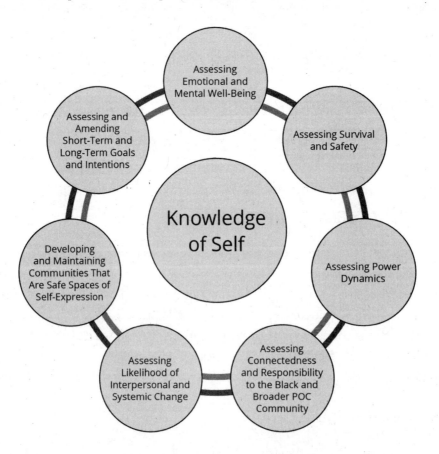

Element	Description
Knowledge of Self	The core of the SNAPS decision making model. This involves deep attunement and understanding of yourself emotionally, mentally, physically, and spiritually, which is an ever-evolving and continuous journey.
Assessing Emotional and Mental Well-Being	Assessing your history of racial trauma, other forms of trauma, and mental health concerns that may impact your capacity to respond to ABR.
Assessing Survival and Safety	The ability to respond to ABR and engage spaces considered unsafe in a way that protects your mental, emotional, physical, and spiritual well-being while also continuing to support your immediate and long-term needs (survival). Psychological and vocational security and well-being in your workplace (safety).
Assessing Power Dynamics	Real or perceived hierarchical privilege based on career position or social identities that impacts the way a person of lesser privilege responds to ABR.
Assessing Connectedness and Responsibility to the Black and Broader POC Community	Our varied degrees of identification and obligation to support and defend the Black and POC community from ABR.
Assessing Likelihood of Interpersonal and Systemic Change	Using experiential, acquired, and historical knowledge (our collective conscious as Black people) of the probable individual, community, and systemic impact of responding to an instance of ABR.
Developing and Maintaining Communities That Are Safe Spaces of Self-Expression	Black spaces, whether familial or chosen, where you feel comfortable to express and be vulnerable about your emotional, mental, and physical reactions to ABR.
Assessing and Amending Short-Term and Long-Term Goals and Intentions	A continuous awareness and ever-evolving inventory of your personal and professional goals in the present and future, including your hopes and expectations for your work experiences that guide your decision making and strategic navigation.

Reflection Questions

1. What components of the SNAPS decision making model are you most curious about? Feel free to mark the areas of the model that you are most interested in learning about.

   _____

   _____

   _____

   _____

2. Are there any aspects of the model that you already incorporate into your decision making when responding to ABR? What have your experiences been like when incorporating these aspects of the model when responding to ABR?

   _____

   _____

   _____

   _____

   _____

The SNAPS decision making is a useful model for deciding how to respond to ABR in the workplace. The subsequent chapters will dive deeper into the model and provide you with opportunities to reflect, learn how the model can be used to strategically navigate ABR, and apply the model to your own life.

CHAPTER 2

The Core of the SNAPS Decision Making Model: Knowledge of Self

In this chapter, you can expect to:

- ✓ Learn how self-knowledge is related to Black psychology

- ✓ Reflect on aspects of yourself that make you who you are

- ✓ Explore how knowing yourself can help you when deciding how to respond to ABR in professional spaces

Knowing yourself means having deep attunement and understanding of yourself emotionally, mentally, physically, and spiritually. It's an ever-evolving and continuous journey that is at the center of strategically navigating anti-Black racism (ABR). *Knowledge of self*, the core of the SNAPS decision making model, involves self-curiosity and using available cultural capital when navigating challenging and harmful spaces. Self-curiosity involves asking yourself questions about what makes you who you are and learning about what you value. Cultural capital refers to the strengths and resources that Black people and other communities of color have to navigate society.

There are six types of cultural capital: (a) aspirational capital (i.e., having hope, despite barriers and challenges); (b) linguistic capital (i.e., knowing multiple languages and/or communication styles, storytelling); (c) familial capital (i.e., family relationships and cultural intuition from ancestors and elders); (d) social capital (i.e., networks and community resources); (e) navigational capital (i.e., knowledge of how to navigate harmful systems and institutions); and (f) resistant capital (i.e., opposing and resisting oppression) (Yosso 2005).

In our society, cultural capital is often not discussed or always seen as a resource. For example, people may make fun of people who speak English as a second language, which may make them feel ashamed about their linguistic capital, but it really is a strength. Additionally, ancestral wisdom like remedies for colds may be dismissed as we matriculate through the formal education system in the United States, but that ancestral wisdom may be valuable as we think about how our ancestors used to heal themselves despite the conditions they faced.

As you become curious about yourself, know that you are not alone and that there is cultural capital that has been invested in you by your community that you can still access by being connected to other people. Oftentimes, the wisdom of our communities is dismissed in professional settings, but knowing who you are and recognizing the strengths of your community can provide valuable resources when navigating ABR in the workplace and supporting your wellness. When your self-knowledge is strong, you have a high degree of self-awareness and mindfulness, and you can use what you know about yourself to assess a situation and make decisions that most align with your authentic self, goals, and values. By having an in-depth understanding of yourself and your identities, you can use knowledge of self to strategically navigate instances of interpersonal ABR in professional spaces.

Knowledge of Self and Our African Roots

You may be saying to yourself, "Of course, I know who I am." But I would challenge you to ask yourself if you know who you are outside what our white supremacist and capitalistic society told you that you could be and are. Most of us don't and that makes sense because that is how we have been socialized.

Think about when you meet someone new whether at work or elsewhere. How do you introduce yourself? Do you start with your name and then mention your job or your education? What are you hoping that people learn about you from how you introduce yourself? When we think about knowing ourselves, it is more than what we do and our achievements—it's about our values, relationships, dreams, purpose, and more.

As a psychologist, I am aware of how Western psychology has historically missed the mark when addressing the needs of Black people and has contributed to the oppression and harm of Black people (Guthrie 2004). Therefore, the SNAPS decision making model is heavily influenced by Black psychology. Black psychology or African-centered psychology is the study of people of African descent and has four core elements: self-knowledge, spirit, interconnectedness, and collectiveness (Parham 2009). Self-knowledge is viewed as vital to a healthy mental state and is reflected in the fundamental questions of Black psychology: *Who am I? Am I who I say I am?* and *Am I all I ought to be?* (Fanon 1967). These fundamental questions encourage deep personal reflection about our character, authenticity, and using our potential. When we think about ourselves in the workplace, we may consider if we are behaving in ways that are authentic to who we are and if we are harnessing our potential.

In a world that often has specific boxes that Black people are supposed to fit in, you may find yourself shrinking who you are, and living in ways that are incongruent with who you are. As you embark on this journey to strategically navigate ABR in professional spaces, it is about more than responding to racist coworkers. This journey and book are for you to take a deep dive into who you are as a person, what your hopes and dreams are, and to feel empowered to make decisions in the face of oppression that most align with who you are and who you want to be.

The core of the SNAPS decision making model mirrors the core elements of Black psychology and an Africentric worldview. In the study that led to the SNAPS decision making model, participants repeatedly mentioned the importance of knowing themselves and how their social identities affected how they experience and respond to ABR. The analysis revealed that knowledge of self was important to participants and informed how they approached the other elements of the model. Further, knowledge of self is a critical first step before any additional action can be taken in support of wellness or to challenge oppression.

You may be wondering, "What should I know about myself?" Well, that is up to you. Ideally, our knowledge of self is a continuous process and we learn about ourselves every day. Racism can often distract or deny us time and energy to engage in continuous exploration of who we are. We are often expected to shift and fit into so many spaces, like our workplaces, that are not ready, capable, or interested in holding the totality of who we are. I encourage you to get curious about yourself. Even if the world cannot appreciate the fullness and beauty of who you are, that does not mean that you cannot continue to explore and celebrate who you are. When we know who we are, we may find it easier to make decisions and choices that are in alignment with who we are and where we want to go in life, which is what the SNAPS decision making model is all about. Let your true inner self lead and guide you as you navigate ABR in the workplace and other challenges.

ACTIVITY
Increasing Your Knowledge of Self: Some Questions to Ask Yourself

Here are some questions that you may want to ask yourself to increase your knowledge of self:

1. Who are you outside of your accomplishments?

    _____

    _____

    _____

2. What identities do you hold dear?

    _____

    _____

    _____

3. What aspects of who you are have been uplifted by yourself and others?

_____

_____

_____

4. What aspects of who you are have been hidden or rejected by yourself and others?

_____

_____

_____

5. What are you passionate about?

_____

_____

_____

6. How would you describe yourself?

_____

_____

_____

7. When is a time that you have been proud of yourself?

_____

_____

_____

8. When is a time that you have been disappointed?

_____

_____

_____

9. What aspects of yourself and your life do you think you could have more grace and understanding with?

_____

_____

_____

10. What do you love most about yourself and most about being Black?

_____

_____

_____

I challenge you to get to know yourself. I challenge you to ask yourself a new question each day or revisit questions where the answer may have changed over time. You are worthy of self-exploration and you are worthy of self-understanding.

Knowledge of self is the core of the model for a reason. Ideally, it is the aspect of the model that you will spend the most time with and refer back to the most because it will influence how you navigate every other part of the model and, ultimately, how you decide to respond to ABR in the workplace. We often know more about the oppressors and their expectations of us than we do ourselves; I implore you to see the value of knowing the fullness of who you are beyond who society has told us we have to be to survive the anti-Blackness we experience.

Knowledge of Self in Action: *Natasha's Story*

Natasha is a lawyer and junior associate at a predominantly white entertainment law company. Natasha oversees a small team of law school interns working on projects for the company. Natasha meets weekly with the other lawyers in her department and the senior lawyer to report on her team's work for the week.

This week, during the weekly meeting, one of Natasha's white colleagues, Dan, commented on Natasha's new hairstyle. Natasha recently got braids and often changes her hair as a form of self-expression. This colleague has made comments about her hair before despite Natasha looking less than thrilled to respond.

As the meeting continues, Natasha reflects on how she can respond in a way that aligns with who she is and who she wants to be. Growing up, Natasha loved styling her hair and changing her look. She comes from a long line of women who have been hair stylists informally or formally in her community. With every new style, Natasha was able to express her creativity in ways that her academics and career choice did not always allow. However, as Natasha got older, she noticed that non-Black people would often comment on her hair or tell her that her hair was "unprofessional." Natasha eventually found a hairstyle that she liked just enough, but that also was consistent enough not to receive unwanted attention from non-Black people in her workplace. She no longer felt excited when she did her hair and, after speaking with a therapist, she realized that maybe her hair meant more to her than she thought. Natasha also started working on standing up for herself and being more assertive. Recently, she spoke with her therapist about wanting to call out microaggressions she experiences with her colleagues. In other spaces, Natasha has prided herself on addressing ABR, but since she started this new job, she has felt less comfortable doing so because she is the only Black woman who is a junior associate.

At the end of the meeting, Natasha decides that she wants to talk with Dan about his comment. Natasha's work with her therapist and her self-reflection allowed her to recognize the aspects of herself that she is working on and to prioritize an assertive response to Dan's comment about her hairstyle. Natasha pulls Dan to the side and lets him know that his comments about her hair make her uncomfortable. Natasha shares that changing her hair is a way of expressing herself and that bringing attention to every time she changes her hair makes her feel "othered" from the rest of their peers. Natasha lets Dan know that although his intentions may be lighthearted, commenting on Black women's hair has historically been microaggressive and hurtful.

Reflect: What do you think of Natasha's response? How did Natasha's knowledge of self impact how she responded to Dan? How would you have responded using knowledge of self?

_____

_____

_____

_____

Exploring Your Social Identities

One way to increase your knowledge of yourself is to build more awareness of your social identities and the impact your social identities have on the way you see and experience the world. Social identities are characteristics that we and society use to categorize different groups of people. Examples of social identities include race, gender, sexuality, or class. Our social identities involve both how we identify as well as how others identify us. For example, in the United States, certain social identities are ascribed to us by the government or other systems, such as our citizenship status or sex assigned at birth; however, there are also social identities that we may have more autonomy over such as our political affiliation or field of study/work.

Use the table below to list your social identities. Star the aspects of your identity you think about the most. Why do you think about those identities more? How do your other identities influence how you feel and react when you experience ABR? Use the "Other" categories to write in identities that may not be listed that are important to you.

Age	Race	Ethnicity	Nationality	Immigration Status
Class/ Socioeconomic Status	Religion/ Spirituality	Sexuality	Gender Identity	Social Support
Mental Health Status	Body Size	Political Affiliation	Location	Field of Study or Work
Education Status	Family History	Ability Status	Other: _____	Other: _____

Reflection Questions

1. Imagine you've just met someone new. How would you describe yourself in three to five sentences?

_____

_____

_____

2. What would you want to make sure that person learns about you? Why would you want them to know about those aspects of you? What parts of yourself do you typically want to hide? Why would you want to hide those aspects of yourself?

_____

_____

_____

3. Do you think other people would agree with this description of who you are? Your family? Your friends? Your partner? Your colleagues? A stranger? Why do you think they would agree or disagree with this description? What aspects of you do you feel like people notice most or do not see?

_____

_____

_____

4. How satisfied are you with who you are currently (From 1—Not at all to 5—Completely satisfied)? What aspects of yourself are you most proud of? What aspects of yourself do you want to improve?

Satisfaction: _____

_____

_____

_____

=== ACTIVITY ===
Interview Yourself

Take some time to get to know yourself. Use this activity as an opportunity to "interview yourself." Think of yourself as a journalist trying to get all the details about who you are. Ask yourself the hard-hitting questions. Below are some questions to get you started.

Complete this sentence:

_____ is at her/his/their best when _____.
     (your name)

In the moment...

When I experience ABR, I feel _____.

When I experience ABR, I think _____.

When I experience ABR, I do _____.

Afterward...

After experiencing ABR, I feel _____.

After experiencing ABR, I think _____.

After experiencing ABR, I do _____.

After experiencing ABR, I wish I _____.

Many of us have been told our whole lives who we are or have been given a couple of options for who we can be. It takes time to unpack and unlearn these narrow confines of who you can be. Completing this chapter takes time and you may find yourself returning to ask yourself the same questions at different stages of your life—that is okay. This book is about you and your wellness. Yes, we are talking about strategically navigating ABR, but without knowing who you are and what you want, it is really hard to have a strategy. Congratulations on finishing this chapter. Now, we will dive into the other components of the model, starting with assessing emotional and mental well-being.

CHAPTER 3

Assessing Emotional and Mental Well-Being

In this chapter, you can expect to:

- ✓ Learn how to assess your emotional and mental well-being

- ✓ Identify how you can use your assessment of your emotional and mental well-being when deciding how to respond to ABR

- ✓ Understand and explore the impact of vicarious trauma on your emotional and mental well-being

As an extension of knowledge of self, the next section of the model is *assessing emotional and mental well-being*. You can think of this stage as regularly scheduled "check-ups" of your mental health. During your life, you may have varying degrees of emotional and mental well-being based on what is going on in your life. Emotional well-being involves how you are feeling. Our emotions can fluctuate as we face different circumstances and situations. Mental well-being involves your emotions as well as your thoughts and behaviors.

For example, you may have recently started caregiving for a family member, which may involve emotions like sadness about their deteriorating health or joy when they have a good day. Further, you may spend a lot of your time thinking about this person and your new role as a caregiver, which may not allow a lot of room for other thoughts. Your behavior may change as you might spend more time at home and maybe have less time for self-care. In this example, it would be important to assess your emotional and mental well-being especially when deciding how to respond to ABR in your workplace. You may have limited emotional and mental capacity to engage with a perpetrator of ABR and that is important to consider when deciding how to respond. Assessing our emotional and mental well-being is a continuous process that can change as we navigate new life situations and experiences. Therefore, it is important to develop skills related to assessing your emotional and mental well-being.

How to Assess Your Emotional and Mental Well-Being

As we have discussed earlier in the book, ABR can take a psychological toll on us. We can experience hypervigilance, anxiousness, depression, distrust of others, muscle tension, and more after a racist incident (Bryant-Davis and Ocampo 2005; Comas-Díaz, Hall, and Neville 2019). In addition to the impact of experiencing ABR, we have other experiences that may be affecting our mental health and well-being. In my research, I found that when Black people assessed their mental and emotional capacity, they either prioritized a response that focused on protecting their mental health and well-being or felt more compelled to educate or directly respond to the perpetrator. Therefore, our emotional and mental well-being provides valuable information that informs our decision making.

═══════ ACTIVITY ═══════
Get to Know Your Emotions

Some of us may struggle with recognizing certain emotions. By completing this activity, you can start to identify how you experience certain emotions and indicators that you may be feeling these emotions. Think about how these emotions influence your thoughts and behaviors and how they show up in your body. For example, you may not explicitly state that you are feeling stressed, but when you take the time to think about it, you may notice that your jaw is clenched, you are having racing thoughts about all of the things that you need to do, and you are easily agitated. This is likely how you experience stress. By being aware of this, you can better assess your emotional well-being and consider how being stressed may impact your response to ABR in the workplace. Maybe you do not have the energy to explain to your coworkers what they did was anti-Black and recognize that engaging in lengthy discussion with them while you have other tasks to focus on may only increase your stress. By naming and understanding our emotions, we can allow ourselves the space to feel them, explore them, and address them rather than letting them consume us due to not understanding where they are coming from or how they are impacting us.

Use the graphics below to describe how you experience the following emotions. Feel free to use crayons or colored pencils to convey the colors associated with these emotions in the circles. Get creative in drawing how you visualize this emotion. Also, use the lines below to think about how your body feels when you experience this emotion, what thoughts you have when you experience this emotion, and which situations tend to make you feel this emotion. Feel free to also reflect on how these emotions show up in your personal or professional life. The bottom three circles are unlabeled so that you can come up with your own personal emotions to name, illustrate, and write about.

Anger

My body feels _____.

I can feel this emotion in this part of my body: _____.

I think about _____ _____.

Some situations that make me feel this emotion are _____ _____.

Sadness

My body feels _____.

I can feel this emotion in this part of my body: _____.

I think about _____ _____.

Some situations that make me feel this emotion are _____ _____.

Frustration

My body feels _____.

I can feel this emotion in this part of my body: _____.

I think about _____ _____.

Some situations that make me feel this emotion are _____ _____.

Peace

My body feels _____.

I can feel this emotion in this part of my body: _____.

I think about _____ _____.

Some situations that make me feel this emotion are _____ _____.

Happiness

My body feels _____.

I can feel this emotion in this part of my body: _____.

I think about _____ _____.

Some situations that make me feel this emotion are _____ _____.

Satisfaction

My body feels _____.

I can feel this emotion in this part of my body: _____.

I think about _____ _____.

Some situations that make me feel this emotion are _____ _____.

_____   _____   _____

My body feels _____.   My body feels _____.   My body feels _____.

I can feel this emotion in this   I can feel this emotion in this   I can feel this emotion in this
part of my body: _____.   part of my body: _____.   part of my body: _____.

I think about _____   I think about _____   I think about _____

_____.   _____.   _____.

Some situations that make me   Some situations that make me   Some situations that make me
feel this emotion are _____   feel this emotion are _____   feel this emotion are _____

_____.   _____.   _____.

ACTIVITY
Mental Well-Being Check-Up

Think about where you are mentally. What are the things that you find yourself thinking about the most? Have there been any significant changes in your personal or professional life? Use the fill-in-the-blanks to assess your mental well-being and check off the mental well-being activities that you have completed or plan to do.

I have been thinking a lot about _____

_____

because _____

_____.

I am looking forward to _____

_____

because _____

_____.

I feel joy about _____

_____

because _____

_____.

I am worried about _____

_____

because _____

_____.

I take care of my physical health by _____

_____.

I take care of my mental health by _____

_____.

I could do a better job of taking care of myself by _____

_____.

Below is a non-exhaustive list of some activities that may support your mental well-being. Check off the activities that you currently engage in and circle activities that you may be interested in incorporating into your life.

- ☐ Spending time doing activities I enjoy

  Activity: _____

  Activity:_____

  Activity:_____

- ☐ Spending time with loved ones

- ☐ Meeting with a licensed mental health professional

- ☐ Meeting with another type of wellness provider (e.g., life coach, spiritual adviser)

- ☐ Exercising

- ☐ Eating healthy foods

- ☐ Journaling

- ☐ Reading self-help/self-improvement books or listening to self-help/self-improvement podcasts or media

- ☐ Relaxing

- ☐ Getting enough sleep

Reflection Questions

How do you assess your emotional and mental well-being? When do you know you need to prioritize your emotional and mental well-being, especially in a situation of ABR?

_____

_____

_____

_____

Using Emotional and Mental Well-Being in Your Decision Making

Assessing your emotional and mental well-being also includes having or developing self-awareness in the face of anti-Black and unsafe spaces to assess your reactions to ABR in the moment and identify the appropriate way to return to equilibrium. Emotional and mental awareness involves deciding the type of response that most honors your emotional and mental well-being. For example, you may feel angry and sad when a coworker makes an anti-Black comment toward you. In that situation, assessing your emotional and mental well-being may involve being cognizant of not reacting based on those emotions in the moment, but still allowing yourself to feel those emotions. You may decide to go to the bathroom or take a walk after the meeting to have a reprieve from the perpetrator of ABR and an opportunity to return to equilibrium.

In situations of ABR in the workplace, sometimes we can recognize our feelings in the moment while simultaneously recognizing that the current environment is an unsafe and unsupportive space for us to express or fully experience those emotions in the moment. *Mindful detachment* is a tool that Black people use in spaces and environments where their feelings are unwelcome and could be considered a liability in the situation. Reacting solely based on emotion is a privilege that historically Black people have not had the opportunity to indulge, which underscores the utility of mindful detachment in the face of strong and valid emotions related to experiencing ABR. It is important for Black people to use self-awareness/mindfulness and emotional regulation when faced with the dysregulating effects of experiences of ABR. Thus, Black people's emotional awareness and regulation can alleviate some of the harmful impacts of ABR (Graham, Calloway, and Roemer 2015).

Black people experiencing ABR often disassociate from their emotions to survive and cope with racial trauma, especially in professional settings (Ashley 2014; Hargons et al. 2022). Dissociating when experiencing ABR can look like going into "autopilot" after a racist incident and moving through the motions of your day without feeling connected to your mind or body. This could also look like avoiding feelings of anger or sadness after a racist incident in a virtual meeting by no longer paying attention to the meeting and mindlessly scrolling social media. However, mindful detachment differs from disassociating from emotions. When using mindful detachment during an ABR experience, you are acknowledging your emotions and recognizing that it is not safe to act on or explore these emotions at the moment. In her chapter "Mindfulness and Matter: The Black Lives Matter Meditation for Healing Racial Trauma," Candice Hargons discussed how mindfulness can aid Black people in reconnecting with their emotions and body rather than feeling compelled to fix themselves or their situations (Hargons 2022). Disconnecting from your emotions and feelings can feel like the best way to ensure your survival and safety, but this decision can also restrict you from making insightful and empowered responses to ABR. Like mindfulness, assessing emotional and mental well-being is an important part of how Black people decide to respond to ABR.

Assessing Emotional and Mental Well-Being and Mindfulness in Action: *Tevon's Story*

Tevon is a Black man and an account manager at a financial services company. He has been working there for six months and this is his first full-time job after graduating with his bachelor's degree in accounting. Tevon is part of a team that works on several high-profile accounts. One of the high-profile clients is a Black-owned tech company, L4, with substantial capital. Tevon is working on an investment proposal for L4. His partner on the project is a Chinese American woman named Sherry. Sherry has made several comments about how she does not know how this company has so much money and has made jokes alluding to the company being a front for drugs. Each time she makes a comment, Tevon ignores her.

Today, Sherry made another comment about the company to Tevon in front of his other colleagues. He noticed that his colleagues laughed. Tevon could feel his skin getting hot and began to clench his fists. Tevon is a taller-than-average Black man and is aware of how it may look if he directly confronts Sherry about her comments. Tevon assesses his emotional and mental well-being by noticing that the culmination of her comments is taking an emotional toll and making him mad. He also decides to engage in mindful detachment until he can get to an emotionally safer setting. Tevon decides to excuse himself from the room and takes his lunch break early. He meets up with one of his Black woman colleagues, Dana, who is on another team, and they go for a walk during lunch. By talking to Dana and engaging in exercise, Tevon notices himself becoming calmer. When he returns to the office, he decides to focus on his presentation with the Black-owned company that afternoon. Tevon shines during the presentation and builds a connection with the CEO of the company. The CEO tells Tevon's boss that he wants Tevon to be the sole account manager for his company's portfolio.

Reflect: What aspects of emotional and mental well-being did Tevon assess? What do you think of Tevon's decision to not directly respond to Sherry? How do you think his decision to focus on his emotional and mental well-being affected his performance during the presentation? What would you have done in the situation?

_____

_____

_____

ACTIVITY
Practice Mindfulness

Tevon was able to use mindfulness in the moment to identify his emotions, seek out an emotionally safe place to express himself, and engage in activities to bring him to the present and calm his rightful anger about the situation so he could decide how to respond.

Mindfulness helps return us to the present and sit with our feelings. Mindfulness looks different for everyone. Try one or more of these activities to explore what aspects of mindfulness you enjoy.

1. Sit with your feet on the ground, back upright, and head facing forward. Close your eyes. Breathe in and out. Repeat three more times. Think of an image that brings you peace—maybe the ocean or clouds passing in the sky. Repeat as you breathe in, "I breathe in love, joy, and liberation." Repeat as you breathe out, "I breathe out anger, frustration, and disappointment." Repeat as you breathe in, "I breathe in acceptance of things I cannot change and strength to fight the things I can." Repeat as you breathe out, "I breathe out what other people have said about me, the hate that comes with racism, the fear that tells me that I am unworthy of better, and the attempts to stifle my voice." Go back to the image that brings you peace and slowly open your eyes.

2. Go for a walk. Rather than focus on your destination, notice the beauty around you. Take time to listen to the sounds that you hear. Look at the people and objects around you. Breathe in the air and feel the wind on your body. What do you notice? Do you see anything in your environment that you haven't noticed before? How do you feel after this walk?

3. Do something creative that aligns with your interests. Write in a journal. Get a coloring book and color. Paint or draw a picture of a scene that brings you joy. Dance to one of your favorite songs.

Reflection Questions

Which mindfulness activity did you try? How did you feel afterward? Do you see yourself using this activity when you experience ABR?

_____

_____

_____

_____

_____

_____

Assessing your emotional and mental well-being allows you to better understand how you are affected by your past and current circumstances and experiences. Being mindful of our mental health can allow us to respond to ABR with consideration for what is best for our well-being at the time. Ideally, we would not have to experience or respond to ABR in the workplace, but by assessing our emotional and mental well-being, we can acknowledge that we are whole people who are allowed to be affected by life and make decisions that respect that reality.

CHAPTER 4

Assessing Survival and Safety

In this chapter, you can expect to:

- ✓ Understand how to assess your survival and safety
- ✓ Make historical connections related to survival and safety
- ✓ Reflect on the wisdom of your ancestors and loved ones related to survival and safety
- ✓ Identify tools and resources that support your survival and safety in your workplace

You are not new to having to respond to ABR in ways that support your survival and safety. This may look like not raising your voice in certain settings because you may be deemed "aggressive" or not sharing your genuine opinion for fear of losing your job. We are constantly evaluating situations to decide what we need to do to survive and support our safety.

My mother, brother, and I lived with my maternal grandparents for a significant portion of my childhood. Therefore, I grew up listening to my grandparents' stories about their experiences. They both lived in the South during Jim Crow and after Jim Crow. I not only often heard about how they had to be vigilant in assessing personal survival and safety but also how they had to *assess survival and safety* in the workplace.

My grandaddy was a very intelligent man. He skipped multiple grades and graduated with a degree in architecture at nineteen years old. My grandaddy joined the army and was an officer. He was constantly having to assess his survival and safety, even around peers. For example, during a firing drill, a white man under his command did not feel that he should have to take orders from a Black man and decided to fire before my grandaddy could get to a safe distance. My grandaddy lost his hearing as a result. My granddaddy was painfully reminded of something he already knew: the lack of safety that he had as a Black man officer during that time.

We may not still be in situations where people feel this comfortable physically hurting us in the workplace, but we may still be surrounded by people who do not believe we should be in our positions. They are also willing to psychologically harm us to exert their anti-Black attitudes. It is important to assess your survival and safety in your workplace so that you will have a fuller picture of your environment and colleagues.

=============== ACTIVITY ===============
Personal Reflection

What does survival mean to you? What has survival looked like for you and those you care about?

_____

_____

_____

How do you define safety? What has safety looked like for you and those you care about? Where do you feel the safest?

_____

_____

_____

_____

Defining Survival and Safety in the SNAPS Decision Making Model

Survival in the SNAPS decision making model means responding to ABR and engaging in potentially unsafe spaces in a way that protects your mental, emotional, physical, and spiritual well-being. It also means supporting both your immediate and long-term needs. *Safety* in the model is psychological and physical well-being as well as career security in your workplace. Lack of safety includes experiences of gaslighting, hierarchical structures that reinforce harm, not being able to trust your peers, and persistent imagined or real fear of retaliation and job insecurity. *Assessing for survival and safety* in your workplace prior to any experiences of ABR can help you anticipate the consequences and discern the best response for you.

A Historical Look at Survival and Safety: We All Have a Role

Assessing survival and safety is not new to Black people. As referenced in the introduction, enslaved Africans took on distinct roles to assess their survival and safety in a new land with a social hierarchy made up of foreign and deadly rules to navigate and survive unsafe and harsh conditions. Molefi Kete Asante, in his contribution to *Four Hundred Souls: A Community History of African America*, described the roles: recorder, interpreter, creator, advancer, maintainer, and memorializer. Despite being from different tribes with diverse cultures, these archetypes were often common threads that enslaved Africans could resonate with and connect to despite language and cultural differences (Asante 2021).

The recorder was tasked with listening and watching everything. The recorder also remembered the collective's secrets and identified themes of the past. The interpreter made sense of the familiar and unfamiliar aspects of enslavement and worked to integrate African values into their new life and brutal reality in the Americas. Creators developed unique ways to navigate slavery that included using their innovative skill sets to address the challenges of enslavement by the Europeans. Advancers took on the task of adjusting African culture and values to the new American society and also worked to secure the rights of enslaved Africans. The maintainer had a clear understanding of society and events, which allowed them to be attuned to and prepared for anything that may come against the collective. Finally, the memorializer took on a spiritual role. They remembered and documented events of the collective and brought out the spiritual aspects of African cultures. These roles were how enslaved Africans survived and created cultures within the Black diaspora that have preserved and infused aspects of diverse African cultures into the new culture that was forced upon them by Europeans and white Americans (Asante 2021). The value of these roles in surviving generations of horrific trauma and experiences is evident in languages such as African American Vernacular English, Gullah, Haitian Creole, Patois, and more.

The ability to work together for the good of the collective is a cultural value in many African cultures and throughout the Black diaspora. Collectivism and recognition of our interconnectedness to each other is how our ancestors survived and it is still important. Hundreds of years later, we still embody the interconnectedness between the individual and community as well as the value of using our strengths to facilitate survival and safety for ourselves and others.

As a result, even today, many Black professionals have a strong knowledge of self and have a willingness to use their strengths to benefit the collective (i.e., the Black community). Some of us have skill sets related to communication and bridging the gap between the Black community and non-Black communities that engage in ABR. Others have skill sets related to self-preservation and emotional and mental survival so that they can have energy to mentor and uplift other Black people entering their field. Others feel that pushing through and surviving anti-Black environments gives them the platform and power to one day change the fields and systems that were so adversarial toward them. For Black people to survive and find some safety in the horrors of slavery and the subsequent eras of oppression, we had to be knowledgeable of our role and use our talents to advance collective survival and safety.

Reflection Questions

1. How would you describe your family's culture? Are there aspects of your culture that you know are related to survival and safety?

_____

_____

_____

2. What have you learned about survival and safety from your elders and ancestors?

_____

_____

_____

═══ ACTIVITY ═══
Write a Letter of Gratitude

Write a letter to your ancestors expressing gratitude for how they survived and other feelings that come up for you. In this letter, also reflect on the lessons you have learned from them and the questions you have for them about navigating anti-Black workplaces. It may feel as though your problems are small compared to theirs, but you may be surprised by the wisdom and knowledge that you can glean from reflecting on the lives of your ancestors and elders.

_____

_____

_____

_____

_____

_____

Assessing Survival and Safety in Action: *Adrian's Story*

Adrian is a Black research scientist. They work for a government research agency that conducts biological science research. Their principal investigator, Dr. Smith, is the leader of the biological science research department of the agency and Adrian's research mentor. Adrian hopes to apply for a promotion that would allow them to start their own research group within the agency. Dr. Smith's research focuses on evolution. Adrian notices that some of Dr. Smith's work has anti-Black undertones. Additionally, Dr. Smith regularly misgenders Adrian, who is nonbinary. Adrian has yet to say anything to Dr. Smith about his research or continuing to misgender Adrian. Adrian began to notice that their chest would tighten when they had to meet with Dr. Smith and that they were starting to avoid their research work altogether.

When Adrian has talked to their coworkers about how hurtful being misgendered and engaging in research with anti-Black undertones is for Adrian, their peers told them that they need to stick it out or they will have a hard time getting a recommendation from Dr. Smith for the promotion.

Adrian recalls a former research scientist and mentee of Dr. Smith's who also was Black and nonbinary—Tate. The research scientist was leaving the agency right when Adrian joined the agency and Dr. Smith's research group, but they were fairly sure that Tate was still in the area. Adrian decides to reach out to the former research scientist. Tate and Adrian meet for coffee.

Adrian shares that they are feeling concerned about the anti-Black undertones of Dr. Smith's research and the work environment. They ask Tate how they handled constant misgendering and conversations about race. Adrian shares that they want to apply for a promotion in the agency so that they could lead their own research group and that Dr. Smith has tremendous influence on promotions as the lead of the research department. Tate shares that they confronted Dr. Smith about his research and asked him to use they/them pronouns when speaking about and to them. Tate shared that Dr. Smith said that he was receptive to Tate's feedback, but when Tate applied for a promotion and other jobs, they found out that Dr. Smith had written a disparaging letter of recommendation for Tate. Tate shared that they have had a hard time finding work within the field because of Dr. Smith's connections within the field. Tate recommended that Adrian not confront Dr. Smith and endure their time under his leadership. Adrian left the meeting feeling uneasy and thinking about the compromises they have already made to "survive" in their research group and the government agency.

Adrian decides to contact human resources as well as send out an agency-wide email, with the support of the Black and LGBTQ+ employee resource groups, critiquing the anti-Blackness in Dr. Smith's research and the discriminatory practices he uses with his employees. The email leads to an agency-wide outcry against Dr. Smith. Demands are made for him to resign despite having over twenty years of service to the agency.

Adrian assessed their survival and safety by recognizing the harmful effects of trying to survive in Dr. Smith's research department, which included the psychological toll of working on research that was being weaponized against the Black community as well as being constantly misgendered. Additionally, *the work environment created by Dr. Smith was affecting Adrian's physical health (i.e., chest tightening and migraines). Adrian decided that surviving in the research group was not sustainable for them and decided to choose psychological safety over surviving in their position in the agency. Although Adrian was unable to continue working in the government agency because of the backlash, they decided to go into the private sector and work at a company that values anti-racist, gender-affirming, and ethical research.*

═ ACTIVITY ═
Reflect on Adrian's Story

What aspects of survival were evident in Adrian's and Tate's stories?

_____

_____

How would you describe the safety within the department culture? What power structures made the environment more or less safe?

_____

_____

_____

How do you think Adrian's other identities influenced how they responded?

_____

_____

_____

What would you have done considering your privileged and oppressed identities?

_____

_____

_____

ACTIVITY
My Workplace First Aid Kit

Imagine that you are creating your own first aid kit for when you need to survive or feel safe in your workplace. What would you put in your first aid kit (both tangible and intangible)? How can you incorporate the components of this first aid kit into your life? Are there any things keeping the components of this first aid kit from being in your life? Some examples may include having a diffuser with calming essential oils (tangible item) in your office or having a set of morning affirmations (intangible) you say to yourself before heading into work that reminds you of your value.

Tangible Items

_____

_____

_____

_____

Intangible Items

_____

_____

_____

_____

Reflection Questions and Activities

1. What have you had to do to "survive" in your workplace?

    _____

    _____

    _____

    _____

2. What would make you feel safe in your workplace?

    _____

    _____

    _____

3. What are things that you can do to make yourself feel somewhat safer in your workplace?

    _____

    _____

    _____

4. Review the roles shared in the historical look at survival and safety section. What role do you see yourself playing in your survival and safety in your workplace? Is there a role that aligns more with who you are that was not mentioned? If so, describe that role.

    _____

    _____

    _____

    _____

    _____

5. Survival and safety are often a collective process in the Black community. Reflect on other Black people in your workplace or field who have skills that can contribute to the collective's survival and safety in your workplace. What do you think it would be like to work with them to support each other's wellness and goals for your careers? Are there barriers that would make that difficult?

_____

_____

_____

_____

_____

Some of you may have been in survival mode for most of your life and it can feel like that's just how life is. As Black people, there are many things that we have survived, and our workplace can be one of those places. I hope that this chapter has allowed you to think about how you can not only have a plan for your survival but also how you can have a space in or outside of the workplace where you feel safe to be all that you are.

CHAPTER 5

Assessing Power Dynamics

In this chapter, you can expect to:

- ✓ Explore how power and powerlessness feel

- ✓ Learn to assess power dynamics in your workplace

- ✓ Identify strategies for strategically navigating power dynamics at work

- ✓ Affirm your inner power at work and outside of work

When Europeans first began to kidnap and enslave Africans, leaders such as Queen Nzinga used their privilege and power to resist and not just secure the freedom of their tribe but of other tribes. Queen Nzinga recognized that she was powerful and was conscious of power dynamics in her interactions with Europeans. In one story, a European leader wanted to speak with Queen Nzinga, but expected her to sit on the floor in front of him (a sign of disrespect). Cognizant of how power was at play, Queen Nzinga strategically asked her servant to get on her knees to form a chair so she was eye-level with the leader (Greene and Mitchell 2021).

Although we all may not be royalty, you may have experienced people, especially non-Black people, who are uplifting themselves while dismissing you. It can hurt when you are made to feel like an add-on to a project or when someone talks over you in a meeting. Unfortunately, in our society, our identities and positions often determine who has power and who does not. This anecdote shows the historical significance of power dynamics when dealing with oppressors and the strategy that is needed to operate from a position of power. Assessing power dynamics includes real or perceived hierarchical privilege based on career position or social identities that impact the way those of lesser privilege respond to ABR. This aspect of the model requires you to have a deep understanding of your social identities, privilege and oppression, and how power works in professional spaces.

=== ACTIVITY ===

Exploring Feelings of Powerlessness in the Workplace

To assess power dynamics in professional spaces, it is important to think about when you feel powerful and powerless. This information can help you think about how to best navigate situations of ABR where you may be in a more powerful or powerless position.

I feel powerless at work when _____

_____

_____

I feel powerful at work when _____

_____

_____

When I work on _____ (task), I feel powerful/powerless (circle) because

_____

_____

When I work on _____ (task), I feel powerful/powerless (circle) because

_____

_____

_____

When I work with _____ (insert name of subordinate, coworker, manager),

I feel powerful/powerless (circle) because _____

_____

_____

When I work with _____ (insert name of subordinate, coworker, manager),

I feel powerful/powerless (circle) because _____

_____

_____

The 4 Ps: Political and Psychological Power and Privilege

Power is when someone has the ability to control or influence other people. Those with power are able to impact the lives of others and therefore affect the trajectory of society. History shows that many wars have been fought to obtain or protect power.

When we think about what it means to be Black in the United States, power is no different. White people, through genocide, enslavement of others, and war, have been able to attain power and have created a well-oiled machine that maintains their power. This power is passed on from generation to generation and takes many forms. Therefore, although Black people built this country, we have been systematically excluded from accessing power for generations.

Those in power also get to decide what wellness, liberation, and resisting oppression look like. Because our media is mostly controlled by those in power, we are led to believe that wellness and health look like having a thin physique or drinking green smoothies. However, when Black people engage in communal wellness by playing card games with friends or hanging out on the porch, we are called lazy or even criminalized for loitering. When the "founding fathers" wanted liberation from the British, it was called revolutionary, but when the enslaved Africans in Haiti wanted liberation from France, they were ostracized by the world and made to pay France. When the Sons of Liberty dumped tea in the Boston Harbor in protest of unfair taxation, it was called a Boston Tea Party, but when Black people protested the murder of Black people at the hands of police, it was called rioting. Power means that those in power get to live a double standard and make the rules up as they go to suit their needs. They have the privilege to both make the rules and change the rules while being protected from the consequences.

This power and privilege are no different in the workplace. We are both ignored but heavily surveilled. Our wins are ignored, but our humanity is dismissed and mistakes are magnified. Those in power often try to define who we can be and who we are. We are made to feel that we have to fit perfectly into their box—or else. What's the "or else"? Intimidation, silencing, exclusion, career stagnation, being passed over for opportunities, losing your voice, being gossiped about, invalidated, unsupported, and the list goes on. Ironically, the box those in power may want us to fit in was never made for us to fit in and the criteria were never made for us to excel (except at the expense of our wellness). Because those in power often tell us who is worthy of wellness—and considering that this country was built off Black people's labor, exploitation, and limited access to wellness—we often don't qualify for the "wellness package." The box and their expectations were made to keep us out and to maintain white supremacy. So, the answer is not to shrink yourself to fit a box that was created to contain us.

Power is both political and psychological. The political is external to us, but the psychological is internal. That means we can take ownership of our mind. Know that your power does not come from your job and who does or does not see value in you. It comes from within, and it comes from knowing how power works and how to work it to your advantage.

Power in the Workplace

Most workplaces have a formal power structure and an informal power structure. Formal power structures look like hierarchies with subordinates, direct reports, middle management, and executives. This is the type of power that you likely expect at your job where the higher the job title, the more power and responsibility and, usually, compensation. Within these hierarchies, there are different gatekeepers. For example, your manager is likely the person who will discuss your strengths and weaknesses with other managers and their bosses. Therefore, your manager is often the gatekeeper of your access to opportunities like promotions. White culture, which is often the model for US work culture, values "objectivity," but as we discussed, with power, "objectivity" is often based on who has power. Additionally, it is virtually impossible for humans to be completely objective; this is when informal power structures come into play.

Remember the social identities we reflected on in chapter 2? Pull them up as we explore how this can influence power dynamics. So, we have our formal power structure at work, but what happens when people with privileged and oppressed identities are dispersed throughout different parts of the formal power structure? Well, it gets complicated. It no longer is simply who has power and who doesn't. Power can vary based on the social identities of those in positions within the power structure because, remember, ultimately, these systems were created to protect and empower whiteness. White fragility is often a way that whiteness is protected and empowered in organizations. Robin DiAngelo (2011) describes white fragility as a defensive state that white people enter when confronted about racism. This can look like the white person starting to cry when confronted about racist actions or claiming that they are hurt that you would insinuate that they are racist. Due to the ways that white comfort is prioritized within society and oftentimes, in the workplace, white people often invoke white fragility to return to a place of comfort when presented with the uncomfortable reality that they benefit from white supremacy and perpetuate ABR.

Because whiteness is so embedded into our systems, white people can even leverage their power within the workplace while technically being a subordinate. For example, as a Black woman leading a group of summer interns, you may have formal and hierarchal power over the interns. However, an intern who identifies as a white man from a wealthy family with connections to the company's executives may still be able to wield his power from the informal power structure in a way that disempowers you. Additionally, you and another colleague may be in the same position within the formal power structure, but may have vastly different experiences with management due to one of you having more privileged identities.

This can even be present when we are working with other Black people. Kimberlé Crenshaw coined the term *intersectionality*, which describes how our social identities "intersect" to create unique experiences of privilege and oppression. Notably, her observation of legal cases related to Black women experiencing discrimination in the workplace were the inspiration for the term. In one case, she noticed that an employer hired white women and Black men, but not Black women. Therefore, the employer was able to claim that they were not discriminating against women or Black people. However, the identities of being Black and being a woman intersected; Black women experienced a unique oppression that was not fully addressed by focusing only on race or gender identity (Crenshaw 1989).

For example, as an African American (a descendant of enslaved Africans in the United States) who was born female and identifies as a woman, I have oppressed and privileged identities that make my experiences unique. In some situations, I am oppressed because of my race and ethnicity due to the anti-Blackness embedded in the United States's systems. In other situations, my United States citizenship allows me ease of access to certain educational and job opportunities whereas a Black person who is not a US citizen may not have the same access. So, as we think about power in the workplace, it is important that we are cognizant of situations where we have privilege and situations where we are oppressed.

Reflection Questions

1. Refer to the activity in chapter 2. What aspects of your identities give you more or less power in your professional space? Are there any examples of when your identities have influenced how you respond to ABR?

2. What power dynamics are at play in your workplace? In what situations do you feel that you have more or less power?

ACTIVITY
The Unwritten Rules

Your workplace likely has unwritten rules due to the formal and informal power structure. Identifying the unwritten rules provides you with more information about how to navigate power dynamics when responding to ABR in your workplace. What are the unwritten rules? If you were giving someone a real description of how your workplace works and who can and cannot do things, what would you say? Some examples of unwritten rules may be:

1. When white women or non-Black women cry in my workplace, they are absolved of accountability for their actions.

2. When Black men express themselves in my workplace, they are labeled as aggressive or angry.

3. In my workplace, they may say company dinners at the boss's house are optional, but if you want a promotion, you have to go.

4. In my workplace, women are punished for questioning or challenging the decisions of men even if they are working on the same project.

5. In my workplace, everyone knows that entry-level employees are expected to stay after 5 p.m. and work on projects that the higher-ups will take credit for.

_____

_____

_____

_____

ACTIVITY
Power Players

Use the table below to identify the people with power in your workplace. Think about this from a formal and informal power structure perspective. People with formal power may be your direct reports or managers. People without formal power may be entry-level employees, interns, or custodial staff. People with informal power may be people with privileged identities or the people who are gatekeepers of opportunities or make completing a task difficult. An example of informal power may be your boss's secretary, who may not have a lot of power in the formal power structure. However, you may know your boss's secretary is often tasked with delegating work to you and your colleagues, serves as your boss's "eyes and ears," or can make completing tasks difficult.

People with Power	People with Power Sometimes	People Without Power

We Are Stronger Together: Leveraging Power Through Relationships

What is your relationship like with the people that you listed above? Take note of who you have strong relationships with and what category they fall into. How might you leverage these relationships to navigate power dynamics?

For example, if you have a strong relationship with a couple of people with power within your organization, you may want to nurture those relationships and consider if they may be helpful when you are navigating ABR in the workplace. Maybe you are close mostly with people who do not have power in the workplace whether due to hierarchal aspects of your workplace or their social identities. You may be able to build community with them and provide each other with support.

In several places I have worked, I have built strong relationships with the Black women at the front desk. The folks at the front desk often are tasked with doing some of the most difficult tasks in the organization, but often can be ignored or dismissed by those with more formal power in the organization. Strong relationships with others can be built despite oppression when we are able to see each other and validate our humanity. I have worked with Black colleagues where we would have meetings before the meetings and plan out what we were going to say and how we would back each other up and affirm each other's points. In those situations, we were not the most powerful people in the meetings by position or social identities but our collective support of each other and united front were able to challenge those who may have had more power. None of us really had power in the situation and were often drastically underpaid, but we were able to work together to support each other whether it was making sure someone got to rest or backing each other up at a meeting.

How to Have a Meeting Before the Meeting

"Meeting before the meeting" is a strategy that you may find useful for identifying how you and the people you are meeting with will navigate a meeting, event, or other activity where you may be disempowered, dismissed, or denied due to ABR.

- **What are reasons to have a "meeting before the meeting"?** There is a history of you and other people with less power (formal or informal) being dismissed and ignored; you are bringing up a challenging topic and want to underscore the importance of the topic; you want to show that there is energy behind the idea or project; or you are nervous about the reaction of others and want support.

- **Who should be at this meeting before the meeting?** People you trust who will also be a part of the meeting; people who may not be attending the meeting but can provide insight and support to make what you share during the meeting more successful; and people who are not going to tell people outside the meeting what you discussed.

- **What should you discuss?** Discuss the topic you want to share during the meeting; workshop the best ways for you to present the topic; provide space for people to express any feelings about the topic or how meetings have gone in the past; how you all can support each other in the meeting and after the meeting (e.g., going out to eat afterward to decompress and celebrate); who will say what and when (consider everyone's varying degrees of power and privilege); and how to handle pushback from others in the meeting.

- **What else should you consider?** You may want to have this meeting in person in a private space (possibly outside of the office); if hosting the meeting virtually, you may want to use your personal accounts and technology to limit the likelihood of unwanted surveillance from other colleagues and your employers; be strategic and thoughtful about who you invite to the meeting and make sure that there is a mutual trust between participants.

Meeting before the meeting is one example of how you can strategically navigate power dynamics in the workplace through relationships. In my research, Black people often feel most comfortable responding directly to a perpetrator of ABR when they feel that they have power in the situation. For example, Black people often feel more comfortable calling out and directly responding to subordinates and colleagues who engaged in ABR rather than their superiors. This comfort is typically due to being abundantly aware of the potential career-damaging consequences of challenging a superior. You also may feel that you have more power in a situation when you know that you have another job, other means of supporting yourself, or an established reputation in your field. That can take the pressure off the interaction because you are less worried about possibly losing your job or professional retaliation.

You also may feel more comfortable speaking up to those in power when you know you have gained all that you needed from the space and you have options and opportunities beyond your current setting. Thus, building and maintaining your professional network inside and outside of your field is vital. By building a professional network, you can have genuine connections you may be able to reach out to for support or who may be able to support you if you do want to change jobs or are experiencing professional retaliation. As a result, you may feel more empowered and secure to respond to ABR in a way that aligns with your values and goals no matter who the perpetrator is because you are operating from a position of power and access to opportunities beyond your current role.

Black professional organizations like the Association of Black Psychologists, National Society of Black Engineers, National Black Law Students Association, National Association of Black Journalists, and Student National Medical Association provide Black graduate students and professionals with mentorship and professional development opportunities that support them as they navigate predominately white fields. Black professional organizations provide Black professionals with opportunities to gain experiences and connections that will make them feel confident to leave professional spaces that no longer support their mental, emotional, or physical safety. Additionally, there are other organizations for Black people that are not based on professions, like Black sororities and fraternities, social clubs, social justice organizations like the National Association for the Advancement of Colored People or the National Urban League, or religious groups. By joining and participating in these organizations, you can develop strong relationships and connections beyond your workplace that allow you to remain connected to the Black community and better able to respond to instances of interpersonal ABR. We will discuss more about building your relationships and connections to others in chapter 8.

Reflection Questions

What organizations or connections can you make that may make you feel more empowered to directly respond to ABR? How can you build your network so that you are not wholly dependent on your professional environment?

_____

_____

_____

_____

_____

_____

Assessing Power Dynamics in Action: *Iman's Story*

Iman is a Black woman elementary school teacher. She has worked at her current school for two years and has been recognized several times by the school district for her excellence in teaching. During a faculty meeting, Iman's principal announces that she and one other teacher, Rachel, have been nominated for the school district's Early Career Game-Changer award. The award recognizes teachers who go above and beyond in the classroom and engage in instruction that fosters leadership and social justice principles in students. The winner of the award wins a $5,000 prize and an all-expenses-paid field trip for their class. The winners are decided based on evaluations from the principal and a vote from their peers.

A couple of weeks later, Iman is announced as the winner of the award. During the faculty meeting, Rachel shares her disappointment about losing the award to Iman. Rachel says that it is not fair that

Iman keeps winning awards and feels that she is always considered the "social justice" educator just because she is Black. Iman asks Rachel for clarity about her statement and begins to share how Rachel's statement was offensive. Before Iman can finish, Rachel begins to cry and say that she is not racist but she just does not think it is fair for Iman to get special privileges because she is Black. The principal immediately begins to console Rachel and asks Iman to understand how Rachel must feel.

Iman assesses the power dynamics by noticing that Rachel is a white Latina and that the principal and her colleagues seem influenced by Rachel's "white woman tears." Iman is aware of how white woman tears can be weaponized against Black people. Iman is also aware of how her response could be viewed through the "angry Black woman" stereotype. Iman considers how her intersectionality as a Black woman gives her less power in this situation and knows that her principal will see how she responds. Iman also recognizes that she is one of two Black teachers in the school and knows that the principal and other faculty do not recognize the racist undertones in Rachel's statement. Iman decides to wait until Rachel calms down to fully respond to Rachel's anti-Black statement.

When Rachel finishes crying, Iman acknowledges Rachel's feelings, but underscores the accomplishments that Iman has made related to teaching and asks that her accomplishments not be relegated to "just because Iman is Black." Since Rachel has only worked at the school for one year, Iman offers to mentor Rachel in achieving her social justice goals in the classroom and plans to use the relationship to educate Rachel on her anti-Blackness. Iman leaves the meeting feeling frustrated but is proud of how she leveraged her limited power in the situation to acknowledge what was wrong about Rachel's comments while maintaining her reputation and relationship with her principal.

Reflection Questions

1. What do you think of Iman's response?

   _____

   _____

   _____

2. What power dynamics were at play in the situation?

   _____

   _____

   _____

3. Have you ever experienced "white woman tears" when responding to ABR?

_____

_____

_____

4. How may concepts of white fragility complicate how you respond to interpersonal ABR in professional spaces?

_____

_____

_____

5. How would you have responded based on your privileged and oppressed identities?

_____

_____

_____

6. How could Iman use a meeting before the meeting with other trusted colleagues to challenge Rachel's weaponization of white woman tears in the future?

_____

_____

_____

Assessing power dynamics is an important consideration when deciding how to respond to ABR in the workplace. There are many instances where we may be disempowered due to our workplace environment, but it is important to think of ways that we can use our individual and collective strengths to combat the disempowerment we may face. In the following chapter, we will continue to explore how our connectedness to our community can impact our decision making when responding to ABR in the workplace.

CHAPTER 6

Assessing Connectedness and Responsibility to the Black and Broader POC Community

In this chapter, you can expect to:

✓ Define assessing connectedness and responsibility to the Black and broader POC community

✓ Identify where you fall on the individualism to collectivism spectrum

✓ Learn the role that interconnectedness plays in the Black community

✓ Identify your role in the Black community

✓ Identify the pros and cons of POC solidarity

✓ Identify strategies for how to navigate ABR based on your feelings of connectedness and responsibility to the Black and broader POC community

✓ Affirm your value as a member of the Black community

When I reflect on my childhood and growing up as an African American on the tail end of the millennial generation in the United States, I see how individualism (i.e., prioritizing self-reliance and the pursuit of personal goals) and collectivism (i.e., interconnectedness and prioritization of relationships and social harmony) have shaped my approach to life. When we think of the African diaspora, we often think of collectivism. Folks working together to survive and thrive. We may think about how family is broader than the nuclear family that is often praised in Western culture. However, the influence of European colonization and imperialism cannot be dismissed in how individualism is also a part of the African diaspora to varying degrees.

For example, my husband and I are both Black, but different ethnicities. He immigrated to the United States from Haiti as a child whereas I am African American and the descendant of enslaved Africans in the United States. Since we are both a part of the African diaspora, we have some similarities in our approaches to life, but also some differences. Our families and cultures have different perspectives on moving away from home. My husband's family values staying close to family members, so living close to family is often a priority. In my family, we love if we can live close to each other, but that is less of a priority than moving somewhere for school or a job. I have not lived in the state I grew up in since high school. I share this example to underscore how our life experiences and culture can impact our level of connectedness and responsibility to those in our lives and the Black community. As I mention throughout this book, no way is right or wrong, but knowing where you stand can help you make decisions that align with your values and goals.

═══ ACTIVITY ═══
Exploring Your Individualistic and Collectivistic Values

Use the scale to identify whether you agree or disagree with the following statements related to individualism and collectivism, your career goals, and addressing anti-Black racism.

1. My career goals are influenced by my family's (chosen or blood) expectations.

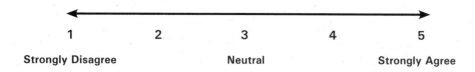

2. I consider how Black people in my workplace will be impacted by my decisions.

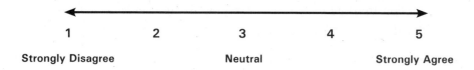

3. If I do not address ABR in the workplace, future Black employees may suffer.

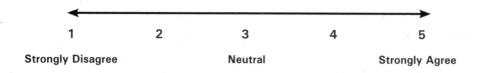

4. I am responsible for making the workplace safer for Black people.

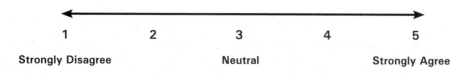

5. My success is tied to the success of other Black people.

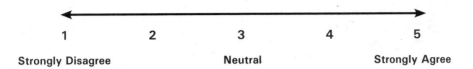

6. I can be most helpful to the Black community by achieving personal success.

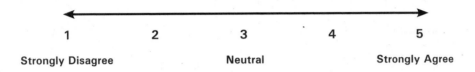

7. Only some Black people can be successful in my workplace.

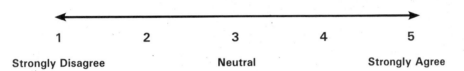

8. I cannot rely on other Black people for support.

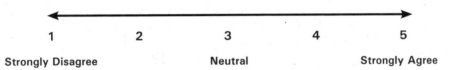

9. When someone is being anti-Black to another Black person, I am unaffected.

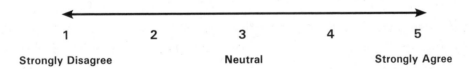

10. I speak up for other Black people even if the anti-Blackness is not directed at me.

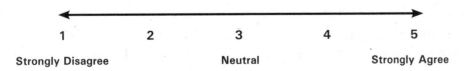

11. I mind my business when a non-Black person says something anti-Black about the Black community.

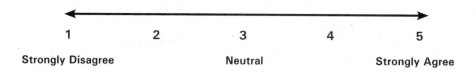

12. I consider a win for another Black person in my workplace to be a win for me.

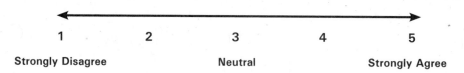

13. Black people in the workplace have to stick together.

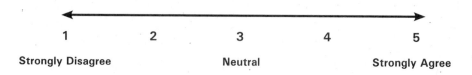

For questions 1–5, 10, 12, and 13, if you put a 4 or more, then you have some collectivist beliefs about your career and addressing ABR. You see yourself as a part of something bigger than yourself and feel that your actions impact the collective. For questions 6–9 and 11, if you put a 4 or more, then you have some individualistic beliefs about your career and addressing ABR. You likely prioritize your personal goals and may think that attaining personal success will allow you more power to make changes later that benefit Black people.

It can be tempting to judge yourself for leaning more toward individualistic views. Black psychology tells us that the collective is important to our personal wellness (Parham 2009). It's hard to imagine that the Black community could survive the continuous assaults on our humanity without being interconnected and maintaining communities of support. However, we also live in an individualistic society and there are benefits to individualistic approaches. As I mention throughout this book, I want you to make decisions that align with your values and allow you to have balance and wellness. If you are surprised by some of your responses or find yourself feeling shame or confusion about why you agreed or disagreed with certain statements, then take some time to reflect on where that shame is coming from and what experiences may have led you to these beliefs.

Black Identity

In addition to understanding your degree of individualism or collectivism, understanding your racial identity can help assess your connectedness and responsibility to the Black community and broader POC community. There are several models of Black identity, but Robert Sellers's Multidimensional Model of Racial Identity underscores how Blackness is not a monolith. Within this model, Sellers presents one dimension known as *racial ideology*. Racial ideology is how a person feels that the Black community should act and respond to anti-Black racism (Sellers et al. 1998). The four ideologies are:

1. Nationalist: focuses on the importance and uniqueness of being a person of African descent.

2. Oppressed Minority: focuses on the overall oppression all marginalized people experience and emphasizes the commonalities Black people have with other oppressed groups.

3. Assimilationist: focuses on similarities between Black people and mainstream American society (white culture).

4. Humanist: focuses on the commonalities of all people, no matter their race.

Reflection Questions

1. Which ideology do you think best describes you? Why?

    _____

    _____

    _____

2. How has your racial ideology changed over time?

    _____

    _____

    _____

3. What experiences have influenced your racial ideology?

    _____

    _____

    _____

4. How do you think your racial ideology determines how you respond to ABR?

    _____

    _____

    _____

Depending on your racial ideology, you may have different views on how others affect your decision on how to respond to ABR in the workplace. Sometimes, we can feel a need to directly address ABR in the workplace not just for our wellness but because we do not want others to deal with the anti-Blackness we are experiencing. This can look like feeling obligated to speak up when a marketing technique for your company is perpetuating anti-Black stereotypes or when you notice there are anti-Black policies at your company that will make it more difficult for Black people in your company to succeed. Sometimes, when you speak up in defense of yourself and other Black people, you experience retaliation, and it may even impact your ability to succeed at the company. It is up to you how much you are willing to risk for the possibility of responding to ABR in a way that can create change for other Black people.

You also may not want to be responsible for addressing issues for all Black people and may want to prioritize your personal goals. This could be because you feel that you can be more helpful by reaching positions of power or maybe you do not feel connected to the Black people in your workplace for whatever reason. It is up to you the level of responsibility you want to take for addressing ABR and how it may impact others. Additionally, for people who identify with the oppressed minority racial ideology, you may feel that you have to respond to ABR in the workplace in ways that not just benefit other Black people but other POC. You may feel that ABR hurts us all and want to make a safer workplace for all POC.

ACTIVITY
Identifying Your Hopes

Think about your hopes for yourself, the Black community, and the broader POC community. Next, organize those hopes into high priority, moderate priority, and low priority. Consider what hopes you are working on in this stage of your life as well as what feels most important to you. Think about how the stage of life you are in, and your life experiences thus far, impact your prioritization.

Hopes for Yourself	Hopes for the Black Community	Hopes for the Broader POC Community

High Priority	Moderate Priority	Low Priority

How might you address when two or more of your high priority hopes conflict with each other?

_____

_____

_____

ABR Perpetrated by Black and Non-Black POC

But what happens when the perpetrator of ABR is Black or a non-Black POC? We can feel disappointed when non-Black POC perpetuate ABR in the workplace. Some of us may feel that non-Black POC can align with whiteness when it benefits them and are not surprised when they perpetrate ABR. Others of us may feel betrayal because they expected other POC to understand the plight of Black people and would want to be on the same team. Black people are not immune from perpetuating ABR in professional settings either. These phenomena underscore the systemic nature of ABR and how looking at ABR and perpetrators of ABR only on the individual level misses the systemic ways ABR impacts all of us. ABR is so pervasive that Black people and other marginalized groups often internalize racism. Internalized racism can be likened to "psychological slavery" and is when oppressed and marginalized groups take on the dominant racial groups' beliefs and stereotypes about the oppressed groups (Akbar 1984; Speight 2007). ABR is engrained in American culture and thus is a part of everyone's daily reality and influences how we view others and ourselves. Hussein Abdilahi Bulhan (1985, 123) describes internalized racism as a "battle on two fronts: the oppressor within and the oppressor without."

Because we know what it is like to live in an anti-Black society, it is valid to have empathy when other Black people or non-Black POC have internalized racist beliefs. It is also valid to feel angry, frustrated, or annoyed. Sometimes, we may respond differently to white people than we would to Black people and non-Black POC. For example, you may be hesitant to call out another Black person for being anti-Black during a work meeting, but may feel more comfortable doing that with a white colleague. I know, for me, I try to avoid talking about "Black business" in front of non-Black people. So, you may decide to pull the Black person aside to share your concerns rather than in a group setting. Maybe with a non-Black POC, you may also pull them to the side and try to see if you all have shared goals related to addressing oppression and express how their intentional or unintentional anti-Blackness does not align with those goals.

Because we share a racial identity with a Black perpetrator of ABR, you may be more compelled to educate them about ABR and share how you were impacted by their actions. Energy is a finite resource, and you may find yourself willing to invest your energy into addressing ABR on a relational level with a Black person or non-Black POC rather than with a white colleague. That does not guarantee that they will be receptive to your response. It is unlikely that you will undo what is likely years of internalized anti-Blackness and racism with a conversation, but you can at least let them know that you know what's happening and that it is unacceptable. Here are some examples of how you might respond to a Black person or non-Black POC who is being anti-Black in the workplace:

1. Can we talk a little bit about what you said during our last meeting? I feel that there are different expectations for Black people because of (insert examples).

2. When you said _____, it seemed to reinforce _____ (insert anti-Black trope). I can imagine that was not your intention but that is how I experienced it and I wonder if other people may interpret it that way.

3. I know that we are all passionate about _____ (example: diversity and equity); however, _____ (insert example) does not seem to align with those values. I'm curious if you feel similarly.

4. As a Black person, I found _____ (insert situation/comment) offensive because _____.

5. It can be really hard being a POC in this workplace. I think it is important that we work together and support each other. I imagine you feel similar. When _____ happened, I felt unsupported because of _____.

These are just some examples of how you might initiate a conversation in response to anyone being anti-Black in the workplace, but especially with Black or non-Black POC because you can try to make connections to some of the shared experiences or goals that you all may have related to racial identity. The best practices section of this book in chapter 11 will also provide additional information about how you can navigate the situation if the conversation does not resolve the issue.

ACTIVITY
Applying Your Connectedness and Responsibility to the Black and Broader POC Community

Read the following scenarios. Think about how you would respond, how your individualistic or collectivistic values may impact your response, and how racial ideology influences your responses.

1. Your coworker, Sarah, is a white woman who is known for giving Black junior associates more difficult projects that often require them to stay late and miss company networking opportunities. You have your own team of junior associates, but notice that in meetings Sarah does not acknowledge the Black junior associates' hard work in their evaluations. You also have seen the non-Black junior associates on her team leave when you leave.

How would you respond?

_____

_____

_____

Which of your hopes for yourself, the Black community, and the broader POC community would influence your response?

_____

_____

_____

Do you think this is an individualistic or collectivistic response? What racial ideology do you think this response most aligns with?

_____

_____

_____

Would you be proud of this response?

_____

_____

_____

2. Your manager, Kenzie, is a Black woman who has offered to mentor you. She has made several comments about how rare it is for a Black person to work at the company and you are beginning to feel like she is in competition with you. During your weekly lunch, she comments on how often your hair changes and that people will not take you seriously if you do not have a more "put together" look.

    How would you respond?

_____

_____

_____

Which of your hopes for yourself, the Black community, and the broader POC community would influence your response?

_____

_____

_____

Do you think this is an individualistic or collectivistic response? What racial ideology do you think this response most aligns with?

_____

_____

_____

Would you be proud of this response?

_____

_____

_____

3. Your coworker, Steve, is an Indian man who recently told you about a new idea that he plans to pitch to your managers. During the conversation, Steve shares that he actually got the idea from a Black man he recently interviewed for an entry-level position at the company. When he sees the concern and confusion on your face, he says, "He's nobody. No one would even believe that some Black guy just starting out came up with this idea. Honestly, he's lucky that someone is doing something with this idea."

    How would you respond?

    _____

    _____

    _____

    Which of your hopes for yourself, the Black community, and the broader POC community would influence your response?

    _____

    _____

    _____

Do you think this is an individualistic or collectivistic response? What racial ideology do you think this response most aligns with?

_____

_____

_____

Would you be proud of this response?

_____

_____

_____

Assessing Connectedness and Responsibility to the Black and Broader POC Community in Action: _Loren's Story_

Loren is a program lead at a nonprofit that provides after school programming for youth in low-income schools. Loren oversees a team of after-school counselors who facilitate programming for the students. She meets weekly with other program leads and the program director to report on her team's work for the week.

This week, Loren and three other program leads are presenting a joint project related to preventing risky behaviors that the program director asked them to work on for him. Loren's collaborators are a white woman, a Japanese man, and a Colombian man. In their meetings for the project, Loren noticed that her collaborators often dismissed her ideas and sometimes talked over her. As they prepared for the meeting, Loren mentioned to her collaborators that she felt that some of the PowerPoint slides negatively portrayed Black people: The slides had pictures of Black people when they were discussing negative behaviors such as substance misuse, drug abuse, and dating violence. However, on the slides talking about positive behaviors, they used pictures of white people. Loren offered to update the slides and switched out some of the pictures on the slides. Over time, Loren noticed that her collaborators would hang out with each other when she was not around. During the meeting with the program director, Loren noticed that her group members pulled up different slides that did not have Loren's updates. Additionally, Loren's collaborators actually included more slides that reinforced negative stereotypes about Black people.

At the end of the presentation, another program lead (not a part of the team) praised them on their presentation. The program director also praised their presentation and asked each person who was a part of the presentation to reflect on the project and their experience working with each other. The program director told the group that they must be so proud and no one seemed to notice the negative portrayals of Black people on the slides. Each of the group members shared that they really enjoyed working on the project and were proud of the work they were all able to do together. Each group member thanked the others for their contributions to the project, but left Loren out of their praises and comments. The program director then asked if Loren had any comments that she would like to share about working with the group and her opinion of the presentation. Loren quickly shared that she enjoyed working on the project and looks forward to how the organization can continue to think critically about how they present difficult topics to students.

Loren assessed her connectedness and responsibility to the Black and broader POC community by recognizing that she entered the nonprofit sector to support Black and other marginalized communities. Therefore, she felt compelled to further address the ABR in the presentation and the lack of respect for her feedback. Additionally, Loren knows that the other program leads work with Black students at their schools and lead teams with Black after school counselors. Therefore, after the larger meeting with the program director, Loren decided to have a meeting with her group members to explain how the presentation was anti-Black and connected the problems with the presentation to the anti-racism and social justice values of the organization.

Reflect: How did Loren's connectedness and responsibility to the Black community impact her response? How would you have responded? How would you describe your responsibility to the Black and broader POC community?

Reflection Questions

1. Who are some people that have inspired you to pursue the field that you are in? What are your hopes and dreams for the Black and broader POC community? How does that impact how you respond to ABR?

    _____

    _____

    _____

2. In what ways has internalized ABR shown up within you? How have you seen internalized ABR show up for others?

    _____

    _____

    _____

Many of us may have pursued our careers because we have a vision and passion for improving the lives of others. We also likely have some degree of commitment to wanting our professional spaces to be safer for Black people. Assessing your connectedness and responsibility to the Black and broader POC community allows you to make decisions that are in alignment with your values. It can be challenging to balance our personal aspirations and goals with our desire for change that benefits all of us. In the next chapter, we will discuss how we can assess the likelihood of change in our professional spaces and consider how we might want to allocate our energy when we are responding to ABR in the workplace.

CHAPTER 7

Assessing Likelihood of Interpersonal and Systemic Change

In this chapter, you can expect to:

- ✓ Define assessing the likelihood of interpersonal and systemic change when responding to ABR in the workplace

- ✓ Define critical consciousness and understand the concept's relevance to deciding how to respond to ABR in the workplace

- ✓ Identify the systems impacting your wellness as a Black person with privileged and oppressed social identities

- ✓ Identify signs that a person is willing to change related to their ABR

- ✓ Define radical hope and how the concept may impact your decision of how to respond to ABR

- ✓ Identify your radical hopes for your workplace and field

Black people in the United States are in an abusive relationship with white people and the systems that uphold white supremacy. Let me explain: Many of our ancestors were kidnapped and enslaved or were subjected to colonization and imperialism within their own countries. Then, when we were "freed," anti-Black stereotypes were made that perpetuated myths that we were lazy, promiscuous, unintelligent, and immoral to absolve white people and the systems they created of blame because, well, we deserved it. With that in mind, we often must balance an awareness of how embedded ABR is in our society while maintaining hope that we can make change and have a better future than our present.

It's a tricky balance. Assessing the likelihood of interpersonal and systemic change when responding to ABR in the workplace is about taking an assessment using experiential, acquired, and historical knowledge (our collective conscious as Black people) of the probable individual, community, and systemic impact of responding to an instance of ABR. *What change will come from my response and how much does making a change mean to me?* In this chapter, you will assess your desire for interpersonal and systemic change related to ABR in your workplace and also assess the people you work with and your workplace for opportunities or avenues of change that will feel meaningful to you. It is important to also keep in mind your other assessments from previous chapters, like your emotional and mental well-being. We are entering anti-Black spaces with varied levels of trauma, prior mental health diagnoses, and different degrees of capacity to challenge anti-Black individuals and systems. Therefore, you must be cognizant of where you put your energy when experiencing and responding to ABR in professional spaces.

It's Not Your Fault: Critical Consciousness and Resisting Self-Blame

As a therapist, one of the concepts that I often try to incorporate into my work with Black clients is *critical consciousness*. *Critical consciousness* is developing an awareness of the systems of oppression and using that awareness and understanding to resist those systems. The term was first coined by Paulo Freire, a Brazilian educator and scholar, in the 1970s (Freire 1970). Since then, scholars like Della V. Mosley have developed models of critical consciousness focused specifically on anti-Black racism and activism (Mosley et al. 2021). Oftentimes, we can start to blame ourselves consciously or subconsciously for the ABR that we experience. This ties into our abusive relationship with white people and systems that uphold white supremacy; we are often told that we are experiencing oppression because of some deficit within ourselves or our community rather than the reality that there have been hundreds of years of concentrated effort to make sure that Black people en masse do not thrive in this country.

Sometimes, when I offer this explanation to Black people, they can feel like it's making excuses or a way of not taking responsibility for themselves. However, it's quite the opposite. As Black people, we are often figuratively and sometimes literally carrying everyone's stuff. We are carrying our personal experiences, battling anti-Black stereotypes, racial trauma, the harm of systems of oppression, and so much more. It's debilitating and it is not sustainable.

So, it can be helpful to pause and actually sort through the baggage that we are carrying. What is my stuff that I can work on and address? What is other people's stuff that I can't control so I am going to give it back to them rather than carrying it with me? What is something that needs to be addressed collectively? Use the activity to sort through some of the "baggage" that you may be carrying.

═ ACTIVITY ═
Unloading Some Baggage

Let's sort through some of the baggage that you may be carrying with you and sort out who it belongs to. This will help with understanding areas of personal growth, releasing yourself from anti-Black standards that originated from society, and identifying whether these things can be addressed individually, collectively, or systemically. If we do not know whose stuff is whose, then we will struggle to assess the likelihood of interpersonal and systemic change in our workplace because we have a distorted view of how change happens and assume responsibility to change things that individually may not be ours to change. Below are some examples of "baggage" that you may be carrying. Think about your baggage and use the three columns to sort them into "My Stuff," "Black Community Stuff," and "White Supremacy's Stuff." You may have things that fit in multiple categories and that's okay.

Example baggage:

- Feeling ugly because I do not fit the beauty standard (light skin, straight hair, and Eurocentric features): *White Supremacy's Stuff*

- Fear of vulnerability because I was discouraged from expressing myself as a child: *My Stuff*

- Believing that you have to work twice as hard to get half of what white people get: *Black Community Stuff and White Supremacy's Stuff* (*this is something often taught in the Black community, but it comes from the impact of white supremacy on our access to opportunities*)

- Tying my worth to my achievements: *My Stuff*

My Stuff	Black Community's Stuff	White Supremacy's Stuff

Take some time to think about how you may have felt personally responsible or that it was your fault for some of this baggage. How has carrying this baggage and weight affected you? What might it feel like to start carrying your stuff and "giving" white supremacy back its stuff? What might it feel like to know that certain issues the Black community must address together and cannot be fixed by an individual? Applying this in your life could look like taking a moment to recognize when you are starting to internalize the anti-Blackness that you are experiencing. For example, your manager is setting unrealistic standards only for you and not your other non-Black colleagues. Instead of rushing to try and meet their unrealistic expectations and blaming yourself, take some time to release those expectations to white supremacy and not take the blame for something that is not your fault. That might not mean that you won't be held to those expectations by your manager, but at least you know where those expectations are coming from and that if you fail to meet those expectations it is not because of your shortcomings but because of your manager's anti-Blackness. By acknowledging when something is your responsibility, a part of white supremacy, or both, you can better assess how to address the issue. For example, you may want to start documenting your interactions with your manager in case you need to escalate the situation to your manager's boss and want to show a pattern of discriminatory behavior.

Interpersonal Change

Most people do not change unless they want to change. That is an often frustrating reality for most people because that means we cannot control other people and, to a degree, can only be accountable for changing ourselves. When responding to ABR, some people factor in the impact that their response will have on the perpetrator of ABR. This can be useful in determining how much mental, emotional, and physical energy you want to put into the situation. For example, if you know this person has been confronted before about their ABR and has still continued, you might decide to respond differently than if this person has been amenable to feedback about ABR in the past or seems open to learning. In my research, some participants talked about whether the person felt like a "lost cause" or someone worth investing energy and time into educating with the hope that they may not repeat their anti-Black behavior. When we factor in the other components of the SNAPS decision making model, keep in mind that just because a perpetrator of ABR may seem open to feedback and being educated does not mean you have to do that if it will be at the cost of other aspects of your wellness. If you do choose to educate the person, you can also think about ways of educating them that expend the least amount of energy and also provide them with opportunities to learn about how they are perpetuating ABR. In the Anti-Racism Resources to Direct Perpetrators of Anti-Blackness to Review, you can find a list of books and courses that you can share with perpetrators of ABR who are open to learning. By directing them to these resources, you can not only save your own time and energy but also assess their commitment to addressing their anti-Blackness by their willingness to engage in independent study. Many Black scholars have done the work to educate non-Black people about ABR, so there is no reason for you to have to take on that role if you do not want to.

Your relationship with the perpetrator of ABR can also impact how you assess their likelihood of interpersonal change. People who care about us can hurt us. That is the reality of being in relationship with other people. We will likely hurt them, and they will likely hurt us. However, people who care about you will make adjustments and changes to prevent repeating the harm in the future when it is brought to their attention. Therefore, if you have a colleague that you are close to who is perpetuating anti-Blackness toward you, you should be able to communicate how what they did hurt you and then they should make an effort to change their behavior and prevent repeating the harm in the future. If they are not open to doing that, you may want to assess if this is someone that you should be close to and if you may want to change how you engage with them. Below are some questions you may want to ask yourself when assessing the likelihood of interpersonal change based on how you respond:

1.   How did this person respond when you shared that their actions or statements were anti-Black?

2.   Did you feel that they were open to how you were affected by the situation?

3.   How did you feel after responding to them?

4.   Did they offer an apology that included taking action to prevent further anti-Blackness?

5.   What is your intuition/gut telling you about this person?

Here are some signs that a person may be willing to address their anti-Blackness:

1.   Acts humbly when told about how their actions affected you or the broader Black community

2.   Listens more than talks

3.   Is open rather than defensive

4.   Decenters themselves and focuses on how you and other Black people were affected

5.   Does not require you to do work for them but takes personal ownership for addressing the anti-Blackness

Reflection Questions

What are some other signs a person is willing to make changes to address their anti-Blackness? What past experiences have you had with people willing to make changes to their anti-Blackness? What past experiences have you had with people who were not willing to make changes to their anti-Blackness? Were there any differences between those people that you noticed that could be helpful to look for?

_____

_____

_____

_____

_____

_____

_____

Read the following scenarios. Assess the perpetrator of ABR's willingness to change and share how you would respond. Please also consider your emotional and mental well-being, survival and safety in the workplace, power dynamics, and connectedness and responsibility to the Black community and broader POC community.

1. Becca is a white, Argentinian woman who you have known for four years. You both started at your job around the same time and often go to work functions together. The other day, she made a comment about how she is almost as dark as you after going on vacation the week before. Later that day, she comments how all the "chocolate" men on the island were so tempting even though she would never take them home to meet her family. Becca is usually supportive when you experience ABR during meetings, but you have noticed that sometimes she equates her ethnicity (Argentinian) to your experiences as a Black person without acknowledging her privilege as a white woman.

_____

_____

_____

2. Stan is a white man from Chicago, Illinois, who is your supervisor. He recently made a comment about how people make everything about race and that he is tired of diversity, equity, and inclusion stuff. Why can't everyone just pull themselves up by their bootstraps like his grandparents who immigrated from Italy? He made this joke after receiving feedback from a higher-up to start considering diversity and inclusion in product development. During the meeting, your colleagues nervously laughed and the comment was not addressed. This is not the first time that he has commented this way; he has been known to be dismissive when people bring up race and often complains that people "just can't take a joke anymore."

_____

_____

_____

These are just a few scenarios to think about how you might assess the likelihood of interpersonal change with a perpetrator of ABR. These situations can be nuanced, but it can be helpful to think about the level of energy you would like to give to the situation and the person's openness to feedback. We also have to consider the systems that can reinforce anti-Black behavior in the workplace.

Systemic Change and Radical Hope

I remember when President Barack Obama was elected. My grandparents and great-grandparents were so elated, and we even got T-shirts with the First Family on them. In my great-grandparents' and grandparents' lifetimes, they saw the end of segregation, had children and grandchildren who attended integrated schools, and saw the first Black man become president. It's safe to say that they saw a lot of systemic change in their lifetime. Conversely, they did see that even with systemic change, anti-Black beliefs and values don't just go away because of new laws and politicians. They saw the impact of the infiltration of Black movements and murders of Black leaders, the 1994 Crime Bill's lasting impact on the mass incarceration of Black people, and the rampant anti-Blackness that President Obama and First Lady Michelle Obama were subjected to on the campaign trail and once they were in the White House.

It can be disheartening to see how anti-Blackness and white supremacy are still so rampant. It can feel suffocating to think about how much energy and effort go into maintaining the status quo. However, like our ancestors, we must hold onto the hope that we can see change in our lifetime. Is the change going to fix everything? Probably not. But I like to think of our hope as Black people as a baton in a relay race. Each generation, we try to run as fast as we can to make the world better, and when it is time, we pass the baton to the next generation, who keep running. Eventually, the race will be won.

When we think about systemic change, we have to know what systems are affecting our wellness. Look at the chart below to see some examples of systems of oppression that you may be navigating. Take some time to look up systems of oppression that you may not be familiar with and fill out the "What Is It" portion of the table. Also, think about how this system is maintained in our society and even some personal examples of how you have seen this system of oppression in your own life.

System of Oppression	What Is It	How It Is Maintained in Society
Anti-Black Racism • Texturism • Featurism • Colorism		
Classism		
Sexism		
Heterosexism		
Transphobia		

System of Oppression	What Is It	How It Is Maintained in Society
Ableism		
Ageism		
Religious Hegemony		

Are there other systems of oppression that are not included in this chart? What are they and how are they maintained within society?

_____

_____

_____

_____

_____

_____

Reflection Questions

We can often be so busy trying to survive and navigate the world we live in that we do not take time to notice the change that we have seen over our lifetime. Reflecting on the change you have seen in your lifetime can help you feel more hopeful about the change that can come in the future. You can think of examples that are personal to you or that you have seen within your community and society. Choose at least three systems of oppression to reflect on and use the "Other" prompt if you would like to reflect on a system of oppression that is not listed.

Example

Texturism: When I was growing up, there were not a lot of natural hair products. Due to my coarse hair texture, it almost felt like my only option was to get a relaxer when I was in elementary school because it was getting difficult to manage my hair. My hair broke a lot of combs. Now as an adult, I have natural hair and there are a lot of products for my natural hair. I still experience texturism when I go to certain hair salons, but I have a lot more options for my hair than when I was a child.

1. Anti-Black Racism

   Change over time: _____

   _____

2. Classism

   Change over time:_____

   _____

3. Sexism

   Change over time:_____

   _____

4. Heterosexism

   Change over time:_____

   _____

5. Transphobia

    Change over time:_____

    _____

6. Ableism

    Change over time:_____

    _____

7. Ageism

    Change over time:_____

    _____

8. Religious Hegemony

    Change over time:_____

    _____

9. Other:

    Change over time:_____

    _____

10. Other:

    Change over time:_____

    _____

=== ACTIVITY ===
Intergenerational Reflection

If possible, have a conversation with some of the elders in your life. Ask them about how they have seen systems change over time and ask them about their hopes for the future. It also may be nice to hear from the youth. If you work with youth or have some sort of mentorship or familial relationship with youth, ask them about their hopes for the future and what their dreams are for the future. Our elders have lived and seen what is possible. The youth often aren't yet jaded by life and are able to imagine infinite possibilities. You likely are in the middle of the youth and your elders. Hearing their perspectives may help you to see life from a different perspective. Use the lines to jot down notes from the conversation that may be helpful to reflect on when you are feeling weighed down by navigating systems of oppression.

_____

_____

_____

_____

_____

_____

_____

_____

_____

A system that likely affects your daily wellness is capitalism, the economic system the United States is based on. Capitalism emphasizes private ownership and profit. Like any system, capitalism intersects with other systems of oppression like the ones listed in this chapter. Think about the different systems within your workplace. What are the priorities in your workplace? How do things get done?

More than likely, your workplace is heavily influenced by white supremacy culture, which includes (a) perfectionism; (b) sense of urgency; (c) defensiveness; (d) quantity over quality; (e) worship of the written word; (f) paternalism; (g) qualified; (h) either-or thinking; (i) power hoarding; (j) fear of open conflict; (k) individualism; (l) progress is bigger/more; (m) objectivity; and (n) right to comfort (Okun 2021). Please visit Tema Okun's "White Supremacy Culture" website (listed in the Anti-Racism Resources to Direct Perpetrators of Anti-Blackness to Review) for definitions and antidotes to these characteristics. Once I learned about these characteristics, not only could I not unsee them within the workplaces I occupied but also within how I even conceptualized myself and structured my own teams. Think about how each of these characteristics shows up in your workplace. What are folks' reactions when these characteristics are challenged or changed? Who seems open to other ways of doing things? What are other characteristics and systems within your workplace that contribute to anti-Blackness? How do you uphold these characteristics and systems and how do you challenge them?

Assessing Likelihood of Interpersonal and Systemic Change in Action: *Henry's Story*

Henry is a Black man in journalism. He works as a reporter for a national news company. Henry notices that his colleagues keep being promoted despite him being the most experienced and hardworking on his team. Henry has a meeting with his new boss who is a biracial man who is hoping to address the stereotypical portrayals of marginalized groups in the media.

Henry was named after his great-grandfather and was close to him. His great-grandfather would often tell him stories about how he would resist ABR during segregation. Henry's great-grandfather often told Henry that the systems in the United States were not going to change unless you made them change. Henry knew all too well how resistant those in power were to change and how ABR was impacting his professional mobility within the company. Henry assessed the likelihood of interpersonal and systemic change before meeting with his boss by looking at the boss's background and stated interest in addressing racism. Henry also thought about how there are likely structures in place that may limit his new boss's ability to completely eradicate ABR from the workplace. Henry realized that he may be able to connect with his new boss in a way that he had not been able to with other bosses even though there may be limited systemic change.

Henry decided that, during his meeting with his boss, he would ask about his lack of promotion and inquire about what he could do to increase his likelihood of promotion. Henry planned to discuss the boss's goals for the company and how ABR had shown up in the company before the boss started working there. In the end, Henry's boss was open to his feedback about how ABR may be impacting Henry's ability to get a promotion. He shared that he had also had trouble in being acknowledged for his work and experiencing discrimination. He agreed to directly supervise Henry and have a meeting to discuss promotion potential in the next couple of weeks. Henry's boss also decided to start a committee focused on a promotion pipeline for historically underrepresented groups.

Reflection Questions

How did Henry assess the likelihood of interpersonal and systemic change? What indicators do you look for when assessing the likelihood of change based on your response?

_____

_____

_____

_____

_____

_____

As we think about the likelihood of interpersonal and systemic change, we can also think about ways of maintaining radical hope. Radical hope allows us to use aspects of our knowledge of our history of oppression and resistance, ancestral pride, ability to envision new possibilities, and recognition of our purpose in life to maintain hope despite the oppression we experience (French et al. 2020). It can be difficult when we feel like change is not happening quickly enough or that the people around us are not ready to change. Those frustrations are valid, but we can also balance that with the radical hope for a better future knowing the vision and strengths of our ancestors who live within us as well as the power of collective resistance. In the next chapter, we will discuss how developing and maintaining communities of safe self-expression can help us as we strategically navigate ABR in our professional spaces.

CHAPTER 8

Developing and Maintaining Communities That Are Safe Spaces of Self-Expression

In this chapter, you can expect to:

- ✓ Define safe spaces of self-expression
- ✓ Understand the role of safe spaces in the Black community
- ✓ Identify your safe spaces of self-expression
- ✓ Learn ways to maintain your safe spaces of self-expression

Safe spaces of self-expression are Black spaces whether familial or chosen where you can feel comfortable to be vulnerable about your emotional, mental, and physical reactions to experiencing ABR. These spaces typically provide foundational confidence for you and reinforce and remind you of your value from an individual, collective, and ancestral perspective. We can often feel so alone when we experience ABR. Sometimes, we can feel shame about what we are experiencing and are hesitant to share our experiences with others.

However, as someone who has conducted several studies with Black focus group participants and co-led several Black therapy groups, I have observed that many Black people feel relieved and validated when they share their experiences with others. For some of us, our families can be our first experience of safe spaces of self-expression. Your family may have instilled certain values that have given you confidence that you can tap into when you face ABR that can deplete your self-confidence. You may also reach out to them for their feedback and support when you are deciding how to respond or find the time you spend with them as a reprieve from your workplace stress.

Not all of us were born into families that provided that foundational support. However, that does not mean that you cannot have other people in your life who fulfill that role. Chosen family includes people who may not be related to you by blood but provide emotional, mental, and physical support that would be expected of a close relationship. Additionally, there are other relationships like friends, acquaintances, mentors, therapists, colleagues, and more who can provide you with support and reminders of your value as you navigate ABR in your workplace.

Reflection Questions

Think about the people in your life that you feel most supported by. What about them makes you feel supported? How do you support them? Does the relationship feel reciprocal?

_____

_____

_____

_____

_____

Some of us have already established safe spaces of self-expression. However, some of us may struggle to find safe spaces of self-expression, especially spaces to safely discuss experiences of ABR in the workplace. As we get older, it can be hard to build new relationships and maintain old relationships. You may live in a different city than where you grew up or have limited opportunities to meet people. Just because you do not currently have a space for self-expression does not mean that it has to stay that way. Think about potential opportunities where you can meet people and communities where you can be yourself and express yourself. Below are some examples of potential safe spaces for self-expression:

- Group chats with close friends or family

- Social media connections/communities (e.g., Facebook groups)

- Meetups with friends or family

- Exercise partners or groups

- Romantic partner(s)

- Religious/spiritual communities

- Individual or group therapy with a licensed mental health provider

- Social, community, or political organizations (e.g., NAACP, National Urban League, sorority or fraternity chapters)

- Professional organizations (especially affiliate groups with other Black people)*

When you are thinking about an ideal safe space of self-expression, you may want to consider what are some qualities of a space that can make you feel like you can express yourself and discuss issues such as ABR in the workplace. Some qualities of a safe space for self-expression are:

- Private

- Balanced

- Supportive

- Encouraging

- Open-minded

- Restorative

- Re-energizing

What are some other qualities that are important to you?

_____

_____

_____

_____

_____

Ideally, spaces of safe expression are not only places where you can discuss experiences of ABR in professional spaces but also places where you can have a reprieve from the stress of navigating ABR. My college friends are one of my safe spaces of self-expression and when we get together, we can talk about difficult topics like ABR, but we can also have fun dancing to our favorite songs from when we were in college. Also, the people in our safe spaces can remind us of who we are when we are in doubt or are feeling weighed down by the impact of anti-Blackness. After a phone call with my best friend, I usually leave reminded of my inherent value and that other people's anti-Blackness does not make me less than or

---

* Be cognizant of who you can trust when talking about work issues because these are people in your field and may not all be people you can rely on.

undeserving of wellness inside and outside of my workplace. We cannot always control our work environment, but we can try to have people in our lives that build us up and support our authentic selves.

Reflect: If you have a safe space of self-expression, think about how you feel in the space. Here are some questions that may help you evaluate your safe space of self-expression:

1. Can I be myself?

2. Can I be vulnerable about my experiences?

3. Is there space for me to share my successes and feel celebrated?

4. Is there balance between what I give to the space and what I receive from the space?

5. Are there aspects of who I am that I feel less safe sharing in this space? Why is that?

6. What has your experience been discussing topics like anti-Blackness in this space?

Safe Spaces and Third Places: A Historical Perspective

Think about some of your favorite shows about a friend group. Usually, they have a meetup place that is not their house and not their workplace. It's a *third place*. Third places are social spaces outside of your home (first place) and workplace (second place) for you to build community with others (Oldenburg 1999). For example, in *Girlfriends*, Joan, Toni, Lynn, and Maya often hangout at various restaurants as their third place (e.g., 847 and J-Spot). There, the women discuss their personal lives, problem solve, and provide support to each other. As a Black person navigating ABR in the workplace, third places provide you with the opportunity to interact with people outside of your home and workplace who can support and uplift you. In addition to providing places to socialize, third places can be sites of resistance to oppression. During the Civil Rights Movement, third places like churches, temples, community centers, hair salons, and barbershops were sites of organizing for protests, legal action, and overall resistance to Jim Crow and white supremacy. As I have mentioned throughout this book, our ancestors have been navigating and resisting ABR for hundreds of years. We can rely on their strength and wisdom as we navigate ABR and the ways it shows up in our personal and professional lives.

=== ACTIVITY ===
Memory Lane with Your Elders

Reach out to an elder in your life (e.g., family member, mentor, friend, etc.) and ask them if they had third places or places outside of work and what those places were like for them. Ask them about what they used to do there and if they ever used those spaces to discuss experiences of ABR. Take note of any interesting aspects of the conversation and lessons you learned.

_____

_____

_____

_____

_____

So, how can your safe space of self-expression help you with strategically navigating ABR in professional spaces? Below are some ways that you can make use of your safe space of self-expression when experiencing workplace ABR:

1. Vent

2. Receive validation

3. Provide a distraction

4. Strategize

5. Navigate

6. Re-energize

7. Remind you of who you are and your value and humanity

8. Receive advice

9. Learn new ways to navigate the situation or about resources

10. Strategize ways to resist the oppression you are experiencing

Safe spaces of self-expression not only provide you with opportunities to strategically navigate ABR but also remind you that although you may be one of a few in a workplace or have limited people in your workplace that you can connect to, you are not alone and there are people who are willing to support you. We are powerful when we are in community with one another.

Developing and Maintaining Communities That Are Safe Spaces of Self-Expression in Action: *Keisha's Story*

Keisha is a Black, bisexual woman who is a graduate student in engineering. She just started classes at her predominately white university. She is a first-year and new to the town. Keisha has begun to feel isolated in her program and at the university because there are few people with her identities. Keisha attempted to join the Black graduate student organization, but did not feel that her identity as a bisexual woman was welcomed.

Keisha is having difficulty with her cohort members who keep excluding her from group projects. Keisha spends most of her weekends alone in her apartment and it is starting to take a toll on her mental health. Keisha talked to her mother about her frustration, and she suggested that Keisha join a club or group where she could meet other people like her.

A couple of weeks later, Keisha sees a flyer for a Black LGBTQ+ therapy group at her university's counseling center. Keisha decides to attend the first group and leaves the therapy group feeling supported and understood. She decides to keep attending the therapy group and engages in developing and maintaining communities that are safe spaces of self-expression. After the group ends, she stays connected with several other group members. Now when Keisha feels isolated or excluded in her program, she reaches out to her friends that she made through the group and they listen and provide advice about how she can respond to these situations.

Reflect: What do you think about Keisha not connecting with the members of the Black graduate student organization? Have you ever been disappointed when seeking community with other people who shared your identities? How do you keep yourself motivated when you are trying to find communities that are safe spaces for self-expression?

Reflection Questions

1. What communities of safe self-expression are you a part of?

   _____

   _____

   _____

2. What communities of safe self-expression do you wish existed and what do you think is keeping those communities from existing?

   _____

   _____

   _____

Hopefully, this chapter has helped you to think about how you can develop and maintain communities of safe self-expression as well as the personal and professional benefits of these communities. Our community can also remind us of our goals and intentions for our professional spaces and put our experiences into perspective. In the next chapter, we will explore how assessing and amending short-term and long-term goals and intentions can help you when deciding how to respond to ABR in the workplace.

CHAPTER 9

Assessing and Amending Short-Term and Long-Term Goals and Intentions

In this chapter, you can expect to:

✓ Define assessing and amending short-term and long-term goals and intentions

✓ Identify the role of goals and intentions in responding to ABR in the workplace

✓ Think about your short-term and long-term goals for your personal and professional life

✓ Learn ways to respond that may align with your short-term and long-term goals and intentions

For many fields, there are certain pathways to your ultimate goal that are almost unavoidable. This can look like having to receive a certain degree before you can apply for a certain job, passing licensure tests, completing mandatory or highly encouraged internship experiences, and more. These pathways typically build on one another, and if they are not successfully completed, they can get in the way of us achieving our goals. For example, a law student in most states would need to complete law school before they can take the bar exam and work as a lawyer. Therefore, law school is a means to an end to becoming a lawyer.

When we decide how to respond to an experience of ABR in a professional space, we have to consider how long we will be in the space and if this space is vital to our goals and aspirations. In this chapter, we will talk about how we can assess our goals and intentions as well as amend those goals and intentions based on our wellness.

Short-Term and Long-Term Goals and Intentions

A goal is the destination that you are hoping to reach and an intention is how you plan to get to that goal based on certain actions. An example of a goal may be that you would like to be promoted in the next year.

An example of an intention would be completing your company's leadership development program to attain the goal of being promoted. You can think about your goals and intentions in professional spaces based on whether they are short-term or long-term. Short-term goals and intentions are things that can be completed in the near future, which could be in the next couple of weeks, months, or even a year. Long-term goals and intentions are usually things that will take longer to complete and are often comprised of several short-term goals and intentions.

When we are aware of what our goals and intentions are for our personal and professional lives, we can consider those goals and intentions when we are responding to ABR in professional spaces. We may want to consider if the professional space or even relationship with the perpetrator of ABR is likely to impact our short-term and long-term goals and intentions. This will allow you to choose a response that has your wellness and goals in mind and to expend energy in the ways you choose.

Reflection Questions

Think about your goals and intentions for your current workplace. Respond to the following questions:

1. Why do you work at your current workplace?

   _____

   _____

   _____

2. Are you satisfied with the type of work that you are doing? Why or why not?

   _____

   _____

   _____

3. When I wake up and get ready for work, I feel _____.

4. I feel most excited at work when _____

   _____

   _____

ACTIVITY
Identifying Your Goals and Intentions

1. What are your short-term and long-term goals and intentions for your workplace?

    _____

    _____

    _____

    _____

2. Have you had to amend or change your short-term or long-term goals and intentions because of ABR that you have experienced?

    _____

    _____

    _____

    _____

3. How do your goals and intentions impact how you respond to ABR in professional spaces?

    _____

    _____

    _____

    _____

    _____

In the next activity, continue to reflect on how you feel about your workplace.

== ACTIVITY ==
Role(s) and Goals Alignment

Now, think about how your current roles and duties connect to your personal and professional goals. Also, think about how ABR has impacted or could impact your personal and professional goals.

1. Role or Duty in Your Professional Space: _____

    a. Connection to your personal goals: _____

    _____

    b. Connection to your professional goals: _____

    _____

    c. Impact of ABR on this role or duty and your personal or professional goals: _____

    _____

2. Role or Duty in Your Professional Space: _____

    a. Connection to your personal goals: _____

    _____

    b. Connection to your professional goals: _____

    _____

    c. Impact of ABR on this role or duty and your personal or professional goals: _____

    _____

3. Role or Duty in Your Professional Space: _____

    a. Connection to your personal goals: _____

    _____

    b. Connection to your professional goals: _____

    _____

    c. Impact of ABR on this role or duty and your personal or professional goals: _____

    _____

When we decide how to respond to instances of interpersonal ABR, we must assess and amend our short-term and long-term goals and intentions. This means being clear on what we hope to gain from our professional spaces so we can make informed decisions when we respond to interpersonal ABR. For example, some people do not respond to every instance of ABR because they do not plan to stay in that setting for too long. This is another way of assessing one's energy and where energy should be allocated.

ACTIVITY
Energy Budget

Think about the various roles and tasks you have in your personal and professional life. Use the first circle below to draw a pie chart and identify how you currently allocate your energy to the different aspects of your personal and professional life. Use the second circle below to identify how you would like to allocate your energy to the different aspects of your personal and professional life. Think about your short-term and long-term goals. For example, I may spend 50 percent of my time focused on work tasks that are made more difficult by having to educate my colleagues about anti-Blackness along with my other responsibilities. I may want to spend less of my time on work and more time on taking care of my health, which may be where I currently put about 20 percent of my energy. Think about how you can adjust your energy budget to allow for your life to align more with your second circle.

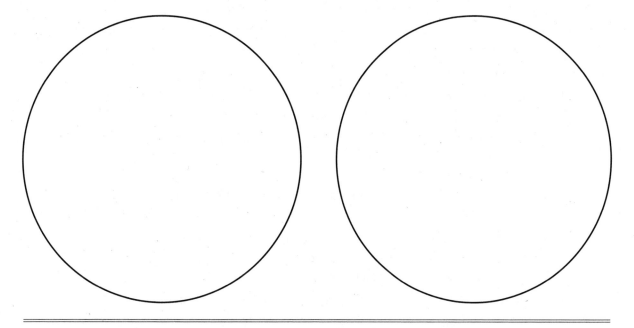

Sometimes, we can be tempted to disregard the impact of the anti-Black incident and act as if it has no effect on us. ABR and racial trauma can consume a considerable amount of an individual's daily functioning and may lead to your goals and intentions being put to the side to confront the persistent threat of ABR and subsequent racial trauma (Bryant-Davis and Ocampo 2005).

So, when you experience ABR in the workplace, where does your energy go? We may be staying up at night ruminating on the situation or struggling to focus on tasks because we are preoccupied with thinking about how we would have liked to respond. It is unrealistic to think that experiencing racism is not going to have an impact on you. Therefore, it may be helpful to be intentional about allocating time and energy to process what happened and to express your feelings about the experience. This could mean adjusting your day, week, or even month to account for time to process your feelings related to the experience of ABR. By allowing yourself time to feel rather than trying to suppress your emotions, you can be mindful of what type of response most aligns with your needs. You may benefit from goal setting throughout your professional journey so you can make sure you are getting the most out of your professional experiences. Continuously checking in and reminding yourself of your goals can help you not become solely consumed with surviving the present situation but also mindful of how you can thrive in or outside of the professional setting.

Assessing and Amending Short-Term and Long-Term Goals and Intentions in Action: *Louis's Story*

Louis is a first generation Haitian American and graduates from medical school next month. Louis flourished in medical school. He received high grades, positive evaluations, and high standardized test scores. Louis has also published two research papers and presented his research on orthopedic surgery at several conferences. Louis also matched into one of the top orthopedic surgery programs in the country and is looking forward to starting the program.

Louis has struggled financially throughout medical school due to the various costs associated with test prep materials, test registrations, and residency application fees. He is unsure of how he will be able to afford moving across the country for his residency program. Louis often sends money back home to his family and also is the primary caretaker for his wife who has lupus. Through the support of a generous donor, the medical school provides one $6,000 scholarship to help graduates with moving expenses related to residency. The scholarship is awarded based on academic achievements, community engagement, and need. Louis's application to the scholarship includes an essay detailing his academic achievements, volunteer work with local organizations, and financial situation.

At the medical school awards banquet, Louis is shocked when his classmate Steve wins the scholarship. Steve is a white man who often bragged about being the son of a prominent physician and living a lavish lifestyle. Steve had less-than-impressive test scores and was known for doing the bare minimum on rotations. Louis is disappointed that he did not receive the scholarship but accepts he was not entitled to win the award and acknowledges that maybe Steve has a financial need that no knows about.

A couple of weeks later, Louis meets with the dean of the medical school, Dr. Brown, for an exit interview about his time in medical school. Dr. Brown asks Louis how he feels about moving and starting residency. Louis shares that he is feeling overwhelmed and unsure about how he will pay for all of his moving expenses. Dr. Brown, who is a middle-aged white man, says that he can imagine Louis was disappointed that he did not win the scholarship but that Louis's "people" are used to working hard and that nowadays there are probably so many other diversity scholarships that Louis could apply to. Dr. Brown says that Steve has an impressive "pull yourself up by your bootstraps" story. Dr. Brown continues to comment on how Steve overcame his low test scores and although he is not as impressive as Louis and does not have financial need, he comes from a long line of doctors and will be an asset to the field. Louis can't help but think that Dr. Brown was not the only person on the scholarship selection committee that felt this way and felt frustrated about how subjective the process seemed to be.

After the meeting, Louis sees his mentor, Dr. Futuro, who asks him how his meeting with Dr. Brown went. Dr. Futuro has been a mentor to Louis and is a fierce advocate for social justice. Louis knows that if he tells Dr. Futuro about his conversation with Dr. Brown, she will likely talk to Dr. Brown about his comments and may encourage Louis to make a formal complaint. Louis has experience with reporting racial bias in the medical school and knows that the process will be lengthy and draining with a minimal likelihood of change. Louis thinks about his energy levels and realizes that he would rather expend energy supporting his wife and preparing to move. Louis also thinks about his long-term goal of becoming a surgeon. Although he is disappointed, he knows that Dr. Brown no longer has the power to impact Louis's goals. He decides not to tell Dr. Futuro about his conversation with Dr. Brown and amends his short-term goals for the summer to include developing relationships with other doctors in the field who he can trust. Louis is rightly frustrated and wants to get Dr. Brown in trouble, but he decides to prioritize his long-term goals by focusing on moving and excelling in his residency program since he is graduating in a couple of days.

Reflection Questions

What are your thoughts about Dr. Brown's "pull yourself up by your bootstraps" comment about Steve? How do you think Louis's other identities played a role in his decision? How would you have responded considering your short-term and long-term goals?

_____

_____

_____

_____

Balancing our goals and intentions with the realities of our workplace environments is difficult. Oftentimes, we may have goals and intentions that conflict with one another and are only made more complicated when we also have to navigate ABR in our professional spaces. This chapter detailed the last component of the SNAPS decision making model. The next chapter explores some of the potential consequences of responding to ABR in professional spaces and details ways that we can anticipate and mitigate these potential consequences.

CHAPTER 10

Anticipating Potential Consequences of Responding

In this chapter, you can expect to:

✓ Learn about three potential consequences of responding to ABR in the workplace

✓ Explore fears and concerns related to potential or experienced consequences of responding to ABR

✓ Identify ways to possibly avoid or mitigate the impact of potential consequences to responding to ABR

One of the most stressful parts about responding to ABR is not knowing what the consequences of your responses may be. This chapter is meant to share some of the common consequences of responding to ABR in professional spaces based on my research. I believe that increasing our awareness of potential consequences when responding can allow us to make informed decisions when responding to ABR and allow us to think about the level of risk we are comfortable taking when we respond. I also want to acknowledge that although white supremacy can act in predictable patterns (e.g., white backlash or "white-lash" to Black progress), it is virtually impossible and unrealistic to get in the mind of a perpetrator of ABR. But we can make use of the resources we do have from other Black people who have been where we are to be aware of potential consequences and outcomes.

The information in this chapter is meant to make you aware of the potential consequences of responding to ABR in professional spaces so that you can make informed decisions. The exercises in each section of the chapter are meant to help you build your "Black wellness insurance." Most of us are expected to have some form of insurance whether it's health insurance, life insurance, car insurance, or any other insurance we pay for in case something happens. So, similar to other forms of insurance, Black wellness insurance is something you pay into with your strategic planning, preparation, and knowledge that these jobs won't save you and, unfortunately, anti-Blackness is pervasive. Black wellness insurance is something to have just in case one of these perceived or experienced consequences happens so that you have set aside resources and ideas in case you need them. I hope that you don't ever have to use this insurance, but if you do, you are prepared.

When I first started my doctoral program, I experienced some ABR in the form of anti-Black stereotypes—the Jezebel stereotype, particularly—being projected onto me. At the time, I was ashamed of my experience and felt too isolated to seek out support from other Black people in the graduate program who were years above me. I wanted to speak up, but I was scared and instead tried to keep my head down. I would spend hours in my apartment spiraling about what would happen if I said anything. I came up with all types of worst-case scenarios because I did not know what the likely consequences were if I said something. I felt like I was the only one and that if I said anything, I would be kicked out of the program.

In reality, I likely would not have been kicked out of the program but may have experienced professional retaliation (which I detail later on in this chapter). I had even considered transferring and that was when I reached out to another Black woman who had transferred programs. I told her a little about the situation and I listened as she told me about the extensive professional retaliation she experienced for leaving her program. I decided to do what felt safest for me at the time: stay in my program and not address the situation.

There were costs and benefits to that decision. Responding to ABR in a way that supports your needs and wellness requires strategic decision making that considers a multitude of factors. Whether you decide to directly confront a perpetrator of ABR or not respond and focus on your wellness privately, that is the best decision you can make at that moment with the information you have available. And that is okay.

Later in my program, a professor changed my grade to a lower grade than I earned. I confronted him with the facts of the situation, and when he still refused to make the change, I went to the department chair and shared what happened. The professor lied and used anti-Black stereotypes to defend why he changed my grade. The department chair eventually changed my grade and was surprised this professor would tell her these untrue things about me and my performance despite evidence proving otherwise.

In that situation, I decided to respond directly to the perpetrator of ABR and inquire about my grade being changed. One of the reasons I felt comfortable doing that was because of discussions with other Black people about their experiences with responding to ABR in the department and me being aware of the potential consequences. I also was more advanced in the program with allies and accomplices and realized that them just kicking me out of the program was unlikely. From my conversations with other Black students and my own interactions, I was aware that the department chair was someone who often would swiftly address ABR and other discrimination. I was able to respond this way because I was aware of most of the potential consequences as well as the pathway of least resistance, which in this case was talking to the department chair rather than going back and forth with this professor.

The Three Potential Consequences of Responding to ABR in Professional Settings

The participants in my research identified three perceived or experienced consequences of responding to ABR in the workplace: (a) financial consequences, (b) professional retaliation, and (c) isolation. Let's review each of these consequences in further detail. As you read through each consequence further, think about if these are consequences you have experienced or seen other people experience when they respond to ABR.

Financial Consequences

Many of us may worry about our job security and financial wellness, especially if we choose to confront a perpetrator of ABR. We may worry about losing our jobs or being passed over for promotions. Financial consequences that could impact loved ones can also be particularly concerning.

For some of us, we may experience the "Black tax," which has a variety of meanings including working twice as hard to get half of what white people get as well as describing the literal additional expenses that Black people pay due to anti-Black systems in the United States. For the purpose of this chapter, I will use the definition of Black tax that has been popularized in South African media and research (Mangoma and Wilson-Prnagley 2019). Black tax refers to the responsibility to financially provide for parents, siblings, and other family members. This can be especially prevalent if you or your parents identify as immigrants, if you are a first-generation college student, or if you are the first person in your family to be middle- to upper-class. Many of us are responsible for people other than ourselves and thus having a job and financial resources is imperative.

We also may be hesitant to label a situation as ABR because we may be comparing our experiences and access to financial resources to previous generations or to what our family's lives were like in another part of the United States or country. From the outside looking in, people in your life may think that you are more financially well off than you are and that can add additional financial pressure when you are perceived that way by people in your life. Thus, the thought of possibly losing your job because of how you responded to an instance of ABR can be scary enough, but even more scary when you know others are depending on you.

If you're an early career professional, you may also have student loans to repay or be just starting in your field and not yet financially stable. You may need to decide on a response that will protect your financial well-being while also addressing any ABR you've experienced. Even if you do not lose your job, there are other challenges that you may encounter professionally depending on how you respond.

=══ ACTIVITY ══=
Keeping Your Options Open

Actively keeping your financial and professional options open can ease some of the financial pressure you can feel when responding to ABR in the workplace. Check off the ways you keep your financial and professional options open and consider if there are other ways of keeping your options open that you may want to explore.

- ☐ Updating your professional social media (e.g., LinkedIn)

- ☐ Attending networking events

  How often?

- ☐ Attending conferences in your field

  What conferences?

- ☐ Joining professional organizations in your field

  What organizations?

- ☐ Seeking out mentors within and outside of your field

- ☐ Keeping your resume/CV up to date

- ☐ Staying connected and maintaining connections with recruiters

- ☐ Consulting a financial planner

- ☐ Identifying potential investment opportunities

- ☐ Budgeting

- ☐ Identifying and setting boundaries related to giving and loaning money to family, friends, and others

- ☐ Contributing to your savings

- ☐ Learning new skills

- ☐ Having a side hustle**

- ☐ _____

- ☐ _____

- ☐ _____

** Be sure to only work on this outside of work hours and be clear on your employer's policies related to outside work.

1. Are you currently satisfied with your financial situation?

   _____

   _____

2. What aspects of your financial situation do you find yourself most stressed about?

   _____

   _____

   _____

3. What aspects of your financial situation are you most proud of?

   _____

   _____

   _____

4. What do you think that you need to feel financially well?

   _____

   _____

   _____

   _____

Professional Retaliation

Professional retaliation can include financial consequences, but expands to affecting your social network and career mobility. Professional retaliation can look like gatekeeping of opportunities, being overlooked for promotions and opportunities, and having a damaged reputation in your field.

Professional reputation is important to many of us and can be particularly important for people at the early stages of their professional identity.

═ ACTIVITY ═
Exploring Your Professional Retaliation Fears

1. What aspects of professional retaliation do you fear the most?

_____

_____

_____

_____

2. How have you seen professional retaliation used in your career or the careers of others?

_____

_____

_____

3. What are some of the specific types of professional retaliation you have seen in your field?

_____

_____

_____

_____

Isolation

In addition to professional retaliation, you may experience isolation and exclusion as a result of how you decide to respond. These experiences of isolation and exclusion can make your work environment hostile and unbearable. I have found isolation to be an insidious consequence that can be present no matter how someone decides to respond to ABR and that can deteriorate your morale and mental health. For many of us, isolation as a Black person in the workplace can be an inescapable reality that we may expect ourselves to be prepared to endure.

Isolation in the workplace can take the form of (a) a continuous experience from the beginning of your employment because of your racial identity or (b) a consequence of deciding to challenge ABR in your professional setting. Isolation in the workplace can be a continuous experience and can look like your coworkers and managers being hesitant or unwilling to make a meaningful connection with you; forming cliques; excluding you from official or unofficial work events where others are able to network and develop meaningful relationships within the company or organization; and expecting you to conform to white cultural norms. Additionally, you may experience isolation after responding to ABR and notice that you are excluded from certain conversations or people are "walking on eggshells" around you. Although sometimes we may wish our coworkers (especially the racist ones) would leave us alone, it can feel unsettling when everyone around you seems connected to one another except for you. We also spend a significant amount of time at work; an uncomfortable and isolating environment can deplete our morale and motivation.

1. Have you experienced isolation in a professional setting? How did you feel and what was the impact on you personally and professionally?

    _____

    _____

2. How have you navigated isolation in the workplace in the past? What have you found helpful and unhelpful?

    _____

    _____

ACTIVITY
Building Your Personal and Professional Community

Take some time to think about your personal and professional community. Having a sense of who you can rely on can help you combat some of the potential backlash you may experience when you respond to ABR in the workplace. List the people in the following categories that make up your professional community. You can also include people that you hope to have in your community. Also, identify the aspects of your life that you feel comfortable sharing with them and areas of your life they can support. For example, you may identify one of your other Black coworkers as a work friend who is able to provide comfort, wisdom, and support related to navigating the company and decompressing from stressful work meetings. We want our relationships to be as reciprocal as possible, so also consider how you may add to their life and opportunities for you to provide support. If you have more than five for each category, feel free to continue this activity in a notebook.

Work Friends or Associates

1. _____

   Areas of comfort, wisdom, and support:

2. _____

   Areas of comfort, wisdom, and support:

3. _____

   Areas of comfort, wisdom, and support:

4. _____

   Areas of comfort, wisdom, and support:

5. _____

   Areas of comfort, wisdom, and support:

Work Mentors

1. _____

   Areas of comfort, wisdom, and support:

2. _____

   Areas of comfort, wisdom, and support:

3. _____

   Areas of comfort, wisdom, and support:

4. _____

   Areas of comfort, wisdom, and support:

5. _____

   Areas of comfort, wisdom, and support:

Friends in Your Field

1. _____

   Areas of comfort, wisdom, and support:

2. _____

   Areas of comfort, wisdom, and support:

3. _____

   Areas of comfort, wisdom, and support:

4. _____

   Areas of comfort, wisdom, and support:

5. _____

   Areas of comfort, wisdom, and support:

Mentors in Your Field

1. _____

   Areas of comfort, wisdom, and support:

2. _____

   Areas of comfort, wisdom, and support:

3. _____

   Areas of comfort, wisdom, and support:

4. _____

   Areas of comfort, wisdom, and support:

5. _____

   Areas of comfort, wisdom, and support:

Friends Outside of Work and Your Field

1. _____

   Areas of comfort, wisdom, and support:

2. _____

   Areas of comfort, wisdom, and support:

3. _____

   Areas of comfort, wisdom, and support:

4. _____

Areas of comfort, wisdom, and support:

5. _____

Areas of comfort, wisdom, and support:

Mentors Outside of Work and Your Field

1. _____

Areas of comfort, wisdom, and support:

2. _____

Areas of comfort, wisdom, and support:

3. _____

Areas of comfort, wisdom, and support:

4. _____

Areas of comfort, wisdom, and support:

5. _____

Areas of comfort, wisdom, and support:

Related and Chosen Family

1. _____

Areas of comfort, wisdom, and support:

2. _____

Areas of comfort, wisdom, and support:

3. _____

Areas of comfort, wisdom, and support:

4. _____

Areas of comfort, wisdom, and support:

5. _____

Areas of comfort, wisdom, and support:

As we have discussed throughout this book, relying on our community can help us as we navigate ABR in professional spaces. We cannot control and may not always be able to predict the potential consequences of responding to ABR, but by knowing who we can depend on, we do not have to deal with these situations alone. It might be helpful when you experience ABR to talk with the people you listed above about the potential consequences and your fears. You all may be able to come up with a plan that best supports you.

Reflection Questions

1. Which of the listed consequences do you find yourself most concerned about when responding to ABR in your professional setting?

   _____

   _____

   _____

   _____

2. What other consequences could there be to how you respond?

   _____

   _____

   _____

   _____

   _____

   _____

=== ACTIVITY ===
Thinking Things Through

Use the activity below to think through the potential consequences of how you decide to respond to interpersonal ABR in a professional setting.

If I respond by doing/saying _____, then _____ may happen. I think that this may happen because of _____. I am preparing for this potential consequence by _____.

If I respond by doing/saying _____, then _____ may happen. I think that this may happen because of _____. I am preparing for this potential consequence by _____.

If I respond by doing/saying _____, then _____ may happen. I think that this may happen because of _____. I am preparing for this potential consequence by _____.

If I respond by doing/saying _____, then _____ may happen. I think that this may happen because of _____. I am preparing for this potential consequence by _____.

If I respond by doing/saying _____, then _____ may happen. I think that this may happen because of _____. I am preparing for this potential consequence by _____.

If I respond by doing/saying _____, then _____ may happen. I think that this may happen because of _____. I am preparing for this potential consequence by _____.

Thinking through the potential consequences of how you respond can allow you to feel prepared when you do respond to a perpetrator of ABR. Sometimes, we can feel nervous or feel that we have to respond in the moment, so taking time to think through your response and consider the possible consequences can allow you to feel prepared for whatever the outcome may be but also grounded in the fact that you are making the best decision after serious consideration. In the next chapter, we will discuss some best practices for responding to ABR, which can be helpful when you are weighing the different potential responses to ABR.

CHAPTER 11

Best Practices for Strategically Navigating ABR in Professional Spaces

In this chapter, you can expect to:

- ✓ Learn about some best practices for strategically navigating ABR in professional spaces

- ✓ Identify other best practices based on your experiences and interactions with other Black people navigating ABR

- ✓ Explore how you might incorporate the best practices identified in this chapter when responding to ABR

In this section, you will find compiled best practices from my research with Black graduate students and early-career professionals about responding to interpersonal ABR in professional spaces. Feel free to take note of the best practices that feel most relevant to you. My hope is that these best practices will add to your toolkit for responding to ABR.

There is so much power in being able to learn from the stories and experiences of other Black people. As a community, we can benefit from the wisdom of others and guidance as we navigate our workplaces. Throughout my life, I have benefited from the mentorship and guidance of other Black people. When you start a new job, if possible, it can be helpful to connect with the other Black people who work there. By connecting with them, you can hopefully feel less isolated, especially in workplaces where white culture is the norm. If you are the only Black person at your job, think back to chapter 8, and seek out communities of safe self-expression outside of your workplace. Additionally, you can learn from each other and provide each other with support when you experience ABR in the workplace. A particularly fond memory of mine is the unofficial practice that the Black people in my graduate program had where the more senior Black students welcomed the incoming Black students and shared with them how to best navigate the program and shared the best practices for getting through the program. I have also experienced similar unofficial practices at my different workplaces. You may find it extremely helpful to learn from others about their best practices for navigating ABR because you can gain insight into potential outcomes and choose the best course of action for you.

Best Practices for Navigating ABR

In my research, the following themes emerged as best practices for navigating ABR in the workplace: evaluate and assess the reactions of others to the anti-Black situation, "take a beat" (i.e., remove yourself from the situation to take a break), be clear on your values and goals, document everything, and use curiosity as a microintervention. Let's take a closer look at each.

Evaluate and Assess the Reactions of Others to the Anti-Black Situation

Evaluating and assessing the reactions of others to anti-Black situations can provide valuable information. It can be helpful to gather as much information as possible about the culture and people in your workplace. If you are a spiritual person or believe in vibes and intuition, you may want to take note of how you feel when you interact with different people and who you feel safe around versus who you distrust. Additionally, when an instance of ABR happens generally or directly to you or someone else, take note of the reactions of others. Notice the people who speak up, the people who avoid addressing the situation, the people who act like nothing happened, and the people who agree. This can provide you with more information about the attitudes and interpersonal styles of the people you work with, which can allow you to identify allies and advocates as well as agents of white supremacy and anti-Blackness. You may find it helpful to first observe others instead of immediately reacting during an instance of ABR. The initial reactions of others can tell you a lot about them and where they stand related to ABR. Your initial observations can inform your response immediately after the incident as well as how you decide to respond in similar situations in the future.

This best practice highlights the importance of identifying trustworthy and harmful colleagues in the workplace. Every moment in your professional setting provides additional data that can help you resist ABR and achieve your goals. This may seem like a lot of extra work, and it is, but remember that oftentimes as Black people we have been socialized to intuitively look for indicators of safety—this is no different. So, trust yourself. Because ABR can be so dysregulating to our mind, body, and spirit, it can be helpful to have the information about who you trust and distrust somewhere accessible, like written in this guide, so that you are not trying to retrieve this information while you are actively in distress due to an anti-Black incident.

Identifying Who Is and Isn't a Good Source of Support

Sometimes, as Zora Neale Hurston would say, "all skinfolk ain't kinfolk," which means that some Black people can be agents of white supremacy and may not treat you like you all are a part of the same community.

We all can have different responses to the ABR that Black people are subjected to, and for some Black people, they may internalize ABR and act in ways that are unsupportive to other Black people. This reality can mean that sometimes receiving mentorship and best practices from the Black people in your workplace may not be an option. It is important to recognize when you are interacting with someone who may have internalized anti-Blackness because they may not be someone that you can seek support from in the workplace. Some characteristics of someone who may *not* be a good mentor or source of support related to navigating ABR are:

1. distances themselves from their Blackness and other Black people;

2. has unrealistic expectations of Black people, different expectations for Black people, or lower expectations for non-Black people;

3. dismissive of conversations about race and racism;

4. individualist in their approach to navigating the workplace dynamics or treats you like competition.

Caveat: Black people having differing or higher expectations of Black people is mainly a concern if the person does not acknowledge how these expectations are unfair. The reality is that there are often unspoken expectations of Black people that are embedded into some workplaces. However, a good mentor will acknowledge that these unrealistic expectations of Black people are rooted in white supremacy and validate how exhausting and distressing this can be.

As we have discussed, Black people can have varied responses to enduring ABR, which are valid because we should not have to be subjected to this treatment in the first place. At the same time, we can have grace and understanding for people who have internalized anti-Blackness while not allowing ourselves to be hurt by their actions or inactions.

On the other hand, here are some characteristics of someone who may be a strong source of support related to navigating ABR:

• Critical and reflective about the impact of ABR in the workplace and beyond

• Open to hearing differing perspectives and experiences, recognizing that your experiences as a Black person and their experiences as a Black person may differ

- Collaborative and open to working together to address issues of ABR

- Willing to use their privilege to advocate for you and others if needed

What are some other characteristics that you would look for in someone who could be a strong source of support related to navigating ABR?

_____

_____

_____

═══════ ACTIVITY ═══════
Identifying Your People

Use this chart to identify people in the workplace who you can count on to act as allies (i.e., non-Black people or Black people with more privileged social identities who are willing to support you) and accomplices (non-Black people or Black people with more privileged social identities who are allies *and* are willing to take risks to support you and change oppressive systems). Bystanders, who arguably through their silence could be categorized as anti-Black, are individuals who have not expressed or shown anti-Blackness but also do not seem interested in addressing anti-Blackness when it comes up and may try to be "neutral." Perpetrators of anti-Blackness are the people who actively do and say anti-Black things and create an anti-Black workplace environment. Also, take note of people you feel less comfortable with or are unsure about where they stand.

Allies	Accomplices	Bystanders	Perpetrators of Anti-Blackness	Unsure

Reflect: What are some specific reactions that you would look for when evaluating and assessing the reactions of others to an anti-Black situation? How would you handle a colleague that you are close to having an unsupportive reaction in an anti-Black situation?

_____

_____

_____

Take a Beat

Taking a beat—removing yourself from the situation—allows for an opportunity to feel your emotions and remove distressing, external variables that are present in an instance of interpersonal ABR. When we experience or witness ABR, we may have visceral reactions. We may feel hot, our muscles may tense up, we might feel uncomfortable in our body, and we may experience anger, sadness, confusion, and more.

Taking a beat allows you to have a private moment outside of a space that expects you to be "professional." As Black people, historically, our raw emotions are often invalidated, pathologized, and dismissed. We can often feel pressure to immediately respond when someone says something racist. In our workplaces, we often have to balance our valid anger, frustration, sadness, and more when we experience or witness ABR within the confines of "professionalism." Professionalism can often be weaponized in the workplace and can feel like a moving goal post. We also are often not in the majority in our workplaces and our colleagues and superiors may weaponize "professionalism" when we express our raw emotions about ABR. This does not mean your feelings are not valid; the workplace is usually not a safe space that is able to hold and support your very real and appropriate feelings. In systems like workplace culture, anti-Blackness can be more of the norm than Black people's reactions to anti-Blackness and thus, taking a beat may allow you to have even a short moment of safety by yourself before returning to that environment.

For some people, taking a beat can look like excusing yourself from the meeting or situation and going to the bathroom to cry, taking a walk during your lunch break, listening to music, texting in your group chat with friends and family, calling a loved one from your car, or taking the next day off to process what happened.

Additionally, taking a beat can give you some time to evaluate the data that you have collected about your workplace to make a strategic decision on how to respond. Taking a beat can allow you the necessary time to be strategic in your actions. Thus, mindfulness of one's emotions is paramount, so you know when you need to take a beat and regroup.

What do you do when you are overwhelmed in a situation of anti-Black racism? What does/would taking a beat look like for you?

=============== ACTIVITY ===============
Taking a Beat Mindfulness Meditation

Use this mindfulness meditation when you are taking a beat. This can be a short mediation and affirmation you can reference during lunch, in your car, or even after a cry session in the bathroom between meetings. You can download an audio version of this exercise at http://www.newharbinger.com/52939.

Inhale slowly and feel your lungs expand. Take in air from your nose and mouth. Hold and count 1-2-3-4-5. Slowly exhale and feel as your lungs constrict as you release air from your nose and mouth. Repeat this two more times. As you breathe in and out, think or say, "I breathe in the strength and power of my ancestors" and "I breathe out and release the hate and mistreatment directed toward me. It is not mine to hold."

Think about a time when you felt most empowered. Envision what you looked like, who was there, and what you did. Remind yourself that this power and confidence is still within you. Remind yourself that strength is more than enduring trials and tribulations—it is allowing yourself to feel. Feel the emotions from what just happened. Let the anger, confusion, sadness, and frustration flow through you. Tense your muscles, clench your jaw, and if you can, even scream or cry. Take your time feeling these emotions. When you are ready, return to your inhaling and exhaling.

Before you return to the rest of your day, choose one or two of these affirmations to say to yourself.

1. *I am valid in how I feel.*

2. *I am not responsible for racism and someone's inability to see my light.*

3. *I have a purpose and calling in my life.*

4. *I have the power to make decisions that are best for my wellness.*

5. *I am filled with the wisdom, love, and power of the Creator and my ancestors.*

6. *I am more than my job.*

7. *I am more than what others say about me and to me.*

8. *I am deserving of love, wellness, and respect.*

9. *I choose people who choose me.*

10. *I am not defined by other's limited imagination—I define myself.*

Being Clear on Your Values and Goals

You may find it easier to decide how you want to respond by being mindful of your values and goals. Values are like a compass, guiding us in the desired direction of our beliefs, and are distinct from goals. Goals are the specific steps you take to fulfill your values. For instance, you might value financial independence, and to live out this value, you set a goal of paying off your credit card balance each month. You may also value and have a desire for liberation and equity for Black people and other POC, which will likely influence how you decide to respond to ABR in professional spaces.

It is up to you what your values and goals are and it's okay for them to change based on your stage of life and other circumstances. For example, when you first start a job, you may be more focused on your professional career and know that at least two years at your current job can open a wide range of opportunities in the future. Therefore, the way you may choose to respond to an instance of ABR during your first year at the job versus your fourth year may be different. You may also value our interconnectedness as human beings and one of your goals may be to educate people about ABR and the impact of other forms of oppression on others. When you face racism, you may respond by using it as a learning opportunity or getting involved in your organization's diversity and inclusion committee. None of these values or goals are more important than the other, but it can be helpful to be aware of what your values and goals are so that you make decisions in alignment.

We all have different personal and professional values and goals that influence how we decide to respond to instances of interpersonal ABR in professional spaces. A deep understanding of your values and goals during each stage of your life can allow you to prioritize and strategically respond while considering all the likely outcomes of your response.

ACTIVITY
Identifying Your Personal and Professional Values

Circle your personal values and star your professional values. Use the blank sections to write in any values that you feel are missing. For your chosen values, use the space below to reflect on your personal definition of those values and what they look like in your personal and professional life. How do these values impact your decision making when responding to ABR in the workplace?

Altruism	Financial Wellness	Joy	Respect
Authenticity	Friendship	Justice	Rest
Black Liberation	Fun	Leadership	Risk
Career	Future Generations	Loyalty	Safety
Change	Growth	Physical and Mental Health	Service
Community	Honesty	Power	Spirituality and Faith
Fairness	Honor	Practicality	Time
Family	Hope	Resilience	Unity

═══ ACTIVITY ═══
Identifying Your Personal and Professional Goals

Reflect on your personal and professional goals. Ask yourself:

1. How have these goals changed over time? How do these goals align with your values?

    _____

    _____

    _____

    _____

2. Who/what are you feeling most protective of at this stage of your life?

    _____

    _____

    _____

3. How are the significant relationships in your life impacting your personal and professional goals?

    _____

    _____

    _____

    _____

4. How does your stage in your career impact your personal and professional goals?

    _____

    _____

    _____

5. How might these goals influence your decision making when experiencing ABR in the workplace?

_____

_____

_____

_____

_____

By recognizing our values and goals, we can check our desired responses to ABR in the workplace with how they align with and move forward our values and goals. We want to make decisions that align with what is best for us and that are value-based. Keeping track of our values and goals in this book and other areas of personal reflection are great for documenting your thought process and how your decision making may change over time. Next, we will talk about how documenting in other aspects of our lives can be beneficial when responding to ABR.

Documenting Everything

My grandmother, affectionately known as Mom-Mom, instilled in me the power of documentation at a young age. I remember when I became secretary for our church's youth group. My Mom-Mom made sure I was able to take the best notes possible. At that time, I was a little annoyed because she never made any of the other kids in our youth group who were secretaries take such detailed notes. But she told me that documentation, including saving all written communications and detailed notes, can be useful when people try to "change history." She told me that when I got older, I would likely be in places that were not as safe as my all-Black youth group and documentation may be my only saving grace when confronted with shifting stories and racism. Similarly, as an HBCU grad, I learned officially and unofficially (if you know about financial aid, then you know what I mean) to keep track of documents and keep good records, which I can't help but think was because they knew the type of work environment that was waiting for us once we left the comfort of our majority-Black institution.

I was not the only one who learned either through elders or personal experience to document everything. The Black graduate students and early career professionals in my research identified documentation as a pre-incident, during an incident, and post-incident best practice when experiencing ABR. Documentation can include written proof of conversations and interactions (e.g., emails, instant messenger conversations, texts, etc.) with subordinates, colleagues, and superiors. Additionally, journaling and other reflective activities can ensure that you recall specific details of a situation in case you need to escalate the situation and speak with someone else (e.g., manager, human resources, lawyer) about what happened. Documenting everything can be incorporated into your strategic navigation of ABR in professional settings. Rather than being surprised when ABR happens, it may be helpful to assume that you will likely experience ABR and use documentation as a proactive practice that can be a resource when/if it happens.

Tips for Documenting Everything

- Treat your email as though it could be read by anyone at any time. Your other colleagues may use their work email as their personal email, but be cognizant that, in most situations, your work email is the property of your employer.

- BCC or CC your personal email on communications that you want to keep a record of in case you lose access to your work email. You do not have to do this with every email, but it might be helpful if you are experiencing ABR or another form of discrimination via email.

- Take notes during meetings. After meetings, send an email confirming what was discussed.

- After an unsettling or distressing interaction with someone in your workplace, write in your journal (with the time and date) about what happened and how you felt. Keep the journal at home and outside of your workplace.

- Take screenshots of communications and interactions that make you uncomfortable or are anti-Black and save them in a personal folder.

- Depending on the laws of your state, record meetings and interactions you know may become contentious or where anti-Blackness may occur.

Reflect: How have you handled conflict in your workplace? Did documentation play a part in how you responded? What are some other ways of documenting in your workplace setting? When do you know it is time to start documenting interactions with someone?

_____

_____

_____

_____

_____

Using Curiosity as a Microintervention

Microinterventions are everyday responses that targets of ABR or allies can use to counteract the harmful impact of ABR and challenge perpetrators of ABR (Sue et al. 2019). As we have discussed, it can be helpful to "take a beat" and not respond in the moment when there is an instance of interpersonal ABR. However, if you do feel compelled to respond in the moment, using curiosity as a microintervention can challenge the perpetrator and put them on the spot to explain why they said what they said. The objective of using curiosity as a microintervention is to force the perpetrator to reflect on the intention and impact of what they said or did.

Although seemingly simple, curiosity can be used to not only challenge the perpetrator but also signal to those around you that what was done or said was anti-Black and unacceptable. Additionally, by "putting the ball in their court," you have time to think, feel, and collect more information about the situation that can aid you in responding. This in-the-moment and direct response can definitely feel intimidating, especially if you are prone to freezing. It necessitates a degree of comfort with making other people uncomfortable, which comes with practice. Oftentimes, we are left to feel uncomfortable and sit with the difficult feelings that come up when someone is anti-Black. This is a great way to return that discomfort to the perpetrator of ABR and allow them to take accountability for what they said or did. This can also mobilize bystanders to act as allies or accomplices in the situation by illuminating and forcing reflection about what happened.

Example Questions to Ask

- What do you mean by that?

- I'm not sure if I'm following. Can you explain this further?

- How does race or this stereotype fit into the conversation?

- How is the situation different from [insert a situation where a non-Black person was treated preferentially]?

- How does this relate to our values around diversity, equity, and inclusion?

- I want to make sure I heard you correctly. Did you say [repeat what was said]?

Reflect: How do you see yourself using curiosity as a microintervention in an anti-Black situation? What additional questions could you use when talking to a perpetrator of ABR?

_____

_____

_____

_____

This chapter discusses some of the best practices that I have found in my research to be useful in strategically navigating ABR in professional spaces and is an example of the collective wisdom that we have as Black people. I encourage you to keep your own list of best practices and have conversations with the people in your life about their best practices. Together, we can continue to build our toolkit for navigating ABR until Black liberation is realized.

Closing Message

ABR manifests in numerous ways that can be covert or overt. However, no matter the manifestations of ABR, the negative impact it has on Black people is evident. Further, in professional settings, Black graduate students and early-career professionals are especially vulnerable to ABR because of the limited power we have in these settings.

I view the SNAPS decision making model as another tool that we can have to resist ABR. I want to underscore that there is never a "right" response to ABR because we should not have to experience ABR in the first place. I hope that by completing this guide you feel better equipped to make decisions in the face of ABR that align with your values and wellness. You should not have to experience the things that you have experienced, and until we can truly achieve Black liberation, I hope that this decision making model can alleviate some of our suffering in anti-Black spaces.

Developing this model and guide was more than just work—it is a love offering to my fellow Black people who are navigating spaces where we are made to feel unwelcomed and disrespected because of our identities. Despite the ABR we experience, our Blackness and the values that have been passed down through generations are our strengths and are embedded in the development of the SNAPS decision making model. Black people have been resisting oppression for hundreds of years and ABR has taken on many manifestations throughout history. If you are experiencing isolation and feel like no one understands, I hope that this guide has helped to fill in some of the gaps that lack of connection to community can create and is a validating force. You may feel physically or even emotionally alone, but the love and wisdom of your ancestors and our collective Black consciousness flow through your body. No matter what the world may tell us, we are worthy of safety, wellness, and peace. If the world will not give safety, wellness, and peace to us, it is imperative that we strategically navigate this world to create and prioritize it for ourselves.

Further Reading and Additional Resources

Black Psychology

- *Handbook of African American Psychology* edited by Helen A. Neville, Brendesha M. Tynes, and Shawn O. Utsey

- *African American Psychology: From Africa to America* by Faye Z. Belgrave and Kevin W. Allison

- *The Psychology of Blacks: An African-Centered Perspective* by Thomas Parham, Joseph White, and Adisa Ajamu

- Association of Black Psychologists (ABPsi): https://abpsi.org

Black Wellness

- *The Unapologetic Guide to Black Mental Health* by Rheeda Walker

- *Racial Wellness: A Guide to Liberatory Healing for Black, Indigenous, and People of Color* by Jacquelyn Ogorchukwu Iyamah

- Center for Healing Racial Trauma: https://www.centerforhealingracialtrauma.com

- Therapy for Black Girls: https://therapyforblackgirls.com

- Loveland Foundation: https://thelovelandfoundation.org

- Therapy for Black Men: https://therapyforblackmen.org

- National Queer & Trans Therapists of Color Network: https://nqttcn.com/en

Responding to Racism

- *First of All… A Daily Journal for Black Women Who Want to Respond to Racism, But Don't Want to Be Called Angry* by Candice Hargons of the Center for Healing Racial Trauma

- *Microintervention Strategies: What You Can Do to Disarm and Dismantle Individual and Systemic Racism and Bias* by Derald Wing Sue, Cassandra Z. Calle, Narolyn Mendez, Sarah Alsaidi, and Elizabeth Glaeser

Anti-Racism Resources to Direct Perpetrators of Anti-Blackness to Review

Books and Media

- *Me and White Supremacy* by Layla Saad

- *White Fragility* by Robin DiAngelo

- *Race Talk and the Conspiracy of Silence* by Derald Wing Sue

- *Race—The Power of an Illusion* produced by California Newsreel, in association with the Independent Television Service: https://www.racepowerofanillusion.org

- *The 1619 Project* by Nikole Hannah-Jones

- *13th* by Ava DuVernay and Spencer Averick

Websites

- White Supremacy Culture website: https://www.whitesupremacyculture.info

- Academics for Black Survival and Wellness: https://www.academics4blacklives.com /anti-racism-training

- National Museum of African American History and Culture: Talking About Race Web Portal: https://nmaahc.si.edu/about/news/national-museum-african-american-history-and-culture -releases-talking-about-race-web

References

Akbar, N. 1984. *Chains and Images of Psychological Slavery*. Jersey City, NJ: New Mind Productions.

Asante, M. K. 2021. "1624–1629: Africa." In *Four Hundred Souls: A Community History of African America, 1619–2019*, edited by I. X. Kendi and K. N. Blain. New York: One World.

Ashley, W. 2014. "The Angry Black Woman: The Impact of Pejorative Stereotypes on Psychotherapy with Black Women." *Social Work in Public Health* 29(1): 27–34.

Bryant-Davis, T., and C. Ocampo. 2005. "Racist Incident-Based Trauma." *The Counseling Psychologist* 33(4): 479–500.

Bulhan, H. A. 1985. *Frantz Fanon and the Psychology of Oppression*. New York: Plenum.

Carruthers, C. 2018. *Unapologetic: A Black, Queer, and Feminist Mandate for Radical Movements*. Boston: Beacon Press.

Carter, R. T. 2007. "Racism and Psychological and Emotional Injury: Recognizing and Assessing Race-Based Traumatic Stress." *The Counseling Psychologist* 35(1): 13–105.

Comas-Díaz, L., G. N. Hall, and H. A. Neville. 2019. "Racial Trauma: Theory, Research, and Healing: Introduction to the Special Issue." *American Psychologist* 74(1): 1–5.

Crenshaw, K. 1989. "Demarginalizing the Intersection of Race and Sex: A Black Feminist Critique of Antidiscrimination Doctrine, Feminist Theory and Antiracist Politics." *University of Chicago Legal Forum* 1989(1): 139–167.

DiAngelo, R. 2011. "White Fragility. " *International Journal of Critical Pedagogy* 3(3): 54–70.

Dickens, D. D., and E. L. Chavez. 2018. "Navigating the Workplace: The Costs and Benefits of Shifting Identities at Work Among Early Career U.S. Black Women." *Sex Roles* 78(11–12): 760–774.

Fain, K. 2015. *Black Hollywood: From Butlers to Superheroes, The Changing Role of African American Men in the Movies*. New York: Bloomsbury Publishing.

Fanon, F. 1967. *Black Skin, White Masks*. New York: Grove Press.

Freire, P. 1970. *Pedagogy of the Oppressed*. New York: Herder and Herder.

French, B., J. Lewis, D. Mosley, H. Adames, N. Chavez-Dueñas, G. Chen, and H. Neville. 2020. "Toward a Psychological Framework of Radical Healing in Communities of Color." *The Counseling Psychologist* 48(1): 14–46.

Gildersleeve, R. E., N. N. Croom, and P. L. Vasquez. 2011. "'Am I Going Crazy?!': A Critical Race Analysis of Doctoral Education." *Equity & Excellence in Education* 44(1): 93–114.

Gilliam, F. D. 1999. "The 'Welfare Queen' Experiment." *Nieman Reports* 53(2): 49–52.

Glenn, C., and L. Cunningham. 2009. "The Power of Black Magic: The Magical Negro and White Salvation in Film." *Journal of Black Studies* 40(2): 135–152.

Graham, J. R., A. Calloway, and L. Roemer. 2015. "The Buffering Effects of Emotion Regulation in the Relationship Between Experiences of Racism and Anxiety in a Black American Sample." *Cognitive Therapy and Research* 39: 553–563.

Greene, G., and D. H. Mitchell. 2021. "Channeling Queen Nzinga in the Fight Against Dysconsciousness at Historically Black Colleges and Universities." In *Black Mother Educators: Advancing Praxis for Access, Equity, and Achievement*, edited by T. O. Jackson, 101–124. Charlotte, NC: Information Age Publishing.

Guthrie, R. V. 2004. *Even the Rat Was White: A Historical View of Psychology*, 2nd ed. Boston: Pearson.

Hargons, C. 2022. "Mindfulness and Matter: The Black Lives Matter Meditation for Healing Racial Trauma." In *Beyond White Mindfulness*, edited by C. M. Fleming, V. Y. Womack, and J. Proulx, 98–109. New York: Routledge.

Hargons, C. N., N. Malone, M. Chesmore, J. Dogan, J. Stuck, C. Meiler, A. Sanchez, et al. 2022. "'White People Stress Me Out All the Time': Black Students Define Racial Trauma." *Cultural Diversity and Ethnic Minority Psychology* 28(1): 49–57.

Mangoma, A., and A. Wilson-Prangley. 2019. "Black Tax: Understanding the Financial Transfers of the Emerging Black Middle Class." *Development Southern Africa* 36(4): 443–460.

Mosley, D. V., C. N. Hargons, C. Meiller, B. Angyal, P. Wheeler, C. Davis, and D. Stevens-Watkins. 2021. "Critical Consciousness of Anti-Black Racism: A Practical Model to Prevent and Resist Racial Trauma." *Journal of Counseling Psychology* 68(1): 1–16.

Okun, T. 2021. "White Supremacy Culture Characteristics." *White Supremacy Culture*. Accessed September 1, 2023. https://www.whitesupremacyculture.info/characteristics.html.

Oldenburg, R. 1999. *The Great Good Place: Cafes, Coffee Shops, Bookstores, Bars, Hair Salons, and Other Hangouts at the Heart of a Community*. Cambridge, MA: Da Capo Press.

Parham, T. A. 2009. "Foundations for an African American Psychology: Extending Roots to an Ancient Kemetic Past." In *Handbook of African American Psychology*, edited by H. A. Neville, B. M. Tynes, and S. O. Utsey, 3–18. Thousand Oaks, CA: Sage Publications.

Reynolds-Dobbs, W., K. Thomas, and M. Harrison. 2008. "From Mammy to Superwoman: Images That Hinder Black Women's Career Development." *Journal of Career Development* 35(2): 129–150.

Sellers, R. M., M. A. Smith, N. Shelton, S. A. J. Rowley, and T. M. Chavous. 1998. "Multidimensional Model of Racial Identity: A Reconceptualization of African American Racial Identity." *Personality and Social Psychology Review* 2(1): 18–39.

Speight, S. L. 2007. "Internalized Racism: One More Piece of the Puzzle." *The Counseling Psychologist* 35(1): 126–134.

Sue, D. W., S. Alsaidi, M. N. Awad, E. Glaeser, C. Z. Calle, and N. Mendez. 2019. "Disarming Racial Microaggressions: Microintervention Strategies for Targets, White Allies, and Bystanders." *American Psychologist* 74(1): 128–142.

Yosso, T. J. 2005. "Whose Culture Has Capital? A Critical Race Theory Discussion of Community Cultural Wealth." *Race Ethnicity and Education* 8(1): 69–91.

Pearis L. Jean, PhD, is a counseling psychologist, and an assistant professor at Towson University whose work focuses on culturally mindful interventions to support survivors of trauma. Pearis has expertise related to racial trauma, and, in 2020, she cofounded Academics for Black Survival and Wellness, a social justice initiative that provides antiracism trainings and Black wellness experiences. She has received several awards from the American Psychological Association (APA), as well as an award from the Organization for the Study of Communication, Language, and Gender for her social justice advocacy.

Foreword writer **Della V. Mosley, PhD**, cocreates healing and wellness as founder or cofounder of Blafemme Healing, The WELLS Healing Center, Academics for Black Survival and Wellness, and The Radical Healing Collaborative—a mental health group practice.

MORE BOOKS from
NEW HARBINGER PUBLICATIONS

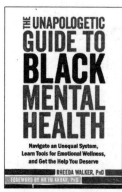

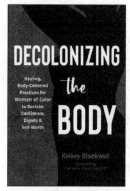

Did you know there are **free tools** you can download for this book?

Free tools are things like **worksheets**, **guided meditation exercises**, and **more** that will help you get the most out of your book.

You can download free tools for this book—whether you bought or borrowed it, in any format, from any source—from the New Harbinger website. All you need is a NewHarbinger.com account. Just use the URL provided in this book to view the free tools that are available for it. Then, click on the "download" button for the free tool you want, and follow the prompts that appear to log in to your NewHarbinger.com account and download the material.

You can also save the free tools for this book to your **Free Tools Library** so you can access them again anytime, just by logging in to your account! Just look for this button on the book's free tools page.

+ Save this to my free tools library

If you need help accessing or downloading free tools, visit **newharbinger.com/faq** or contact us at **customerservice@newharbinger.com**.